A to Z of God's Character

Character

Loving God by Knowing Him More

Sarah Travis

Copyright © 2015 Sarah Travis

All rights reserved.

ISBN: 1519394705
ISBN-13: 978-1519394705

CONTENTS

Introduction   1

Day 1 He is our ALPHA God!   3

Day 2 He is God Almighty!   6

Day 3 God is Beautiful!   8

Day 4 God is Compassionate!   12

Day 5 Creator God!   17

Day 6 God is Divine!   21

Day 7 God is our Deliverer!   23

Day 8 God is Eternal...Everlasting!   26

Day 9 God is Faithful and Forgiving!   29

Day 10 God is Gracious!   34

Day 11 God is Holy, Holy, Holy!   38

Day 12 God is Incomprehensible!   43

Day 13 God is Jealous...Over You!   47

Day 14 God is King of Kings!   52

Day 15 God is Love so gives us Himself!   56

Day 16 He is a Merciful God!   61

Day 17 God Names and ReNames!   65

Day 18 God is Omnipresent!   70

Day 19 God is Omniscient!   73

Day 20 God is Omnipotent!   76

Day 21 God is Perfectly Patient!   79

Day 22 When God is Quiet...   83

Day 23 The Righteousness of God!   89

Day 24 God is Sovereign Over All!   96

Day 25 We Can Trust God because He is True!   101

Day 26 Only our God is Unchanging!   106

Day 27 God's VICTORY is ours to claim!   111

Day 28 He is Worthy of our Praise!   116

Day 29 God is our Xenagogue – Guide!   121

Day 30 Yahweh is who God is!   125

Day 31 God is Zealous for His people!   129

A Prayer and Thank You!   134

About Sarah Travis   137

INTRODUCTION

Over the years I have questioned many aspects of God's character without even realizing it — maybe I'm not alone.

My fears show a lack of trust in His sovereignty and provision.

My continual planning shows a lack of belief in His omniscience ~ He is all knowing.

 When I question why I was placed in a certain situation I am doubting His perfect plan for my life.

When anger rises up in me while watching the heart-wrenching pain of suffering I am putting His lovingkindness into question.

When I hold on to the sin of my past unable to forgive myself I am rejecting His atoning sacrifice, cleansing power and forgiveness.

All of the fears, doubts, questions, and emotions that rise up within me on a daily basis all count down to one common denominator...

They all show a lack of belief in the character of God.

I believe every Bible Study should result in us knowing our Father and His Son Jesus more. He reveals His character to us

1

throughout Scripture and so I invite you to join me as I explore the:

A to Z of God's Character

For 31 days we will study a characteristic beginning with a letter of the alphabet and after each letter {which may span multiple days} there will be a few study questions to take your thinking to a deeper level. There is space to record your thoughts but my suggestion is to grab a journal to accompany you on this journey.

I have also created a playlist in YouTube to reflect on the A to Z of God's Character with a worship song speaking to each characteristic. I suggest you use this playlist to end your time of devotion each day. http://bit.ly/1OYmJIa

Thank you for joining me on this journey!

.

DAY 1: He is our ALPHA God!

What better way to begin a study of the A to Z of God's Character than to look at Him as our:

ALPHA!

Alpha is the first letter in the Greek alphabet and three times in Revelation Jesus says the words:

"I am the Alpha and the Omega" Revelation 1:8, 21:6, and 22:13

In Revelation 21:6 Jesus goes on to say that He is: *"the beginning and the end"*, and in Revelation 22:13: *"the first and the last, the beginning and the end!"*

Let us firstly clarify a foundational Truth — Jesus is God! So, when Jesus describes Himself as *ALPHA* we know we can say that God is *ALPHA!*

In John 1:1 we read:

"In the beginning was the Word, and the Word was with God, and the Word was God." John 1:1 ESV

The Strongs Concordance defines the Greek word used in John 1:1: *"lógos ("word") is pre-eminently used of Christ (Jn 1:1), expressing the thoughts of the Father through the Spirit"*, so John is describing Jesus as being the Word who was present at the beginning of all time and as being God. Further on in John, he records Jesus saying: *"I and the Father are **one**" John 10:30 ESV*

Now we have clarified the truth of God and Jesus being one in the same...we can trust and believe any characteristic describing Jesus can also be used to describe our Father God in Heaven! An important point to understand for the remainder of this study!

God even says in Scripture that He is our A to Z:

> ***"I am the one; I am present at the very beginning and at the very end." Isaiah 48:12b***

God was present before the beginning of time: *"In the beginning, God created the heavens and the earth" Genesis 1:1 ESV.* He was self-existent before *ANYTHING!*

God is the beginning of all things and *"The life of every living thing is in His hand, as well as the breath of all mankind" Job 12:10 HCSB.* All living things begin with God. He created them. He created me. He is the beginning of my life and just as His mercies are brand new every day (Lamentations 3:22-23)...He is the beginning of every day on earth (Psalm 118:24).

So often I wake up in the morning and my mind is racing through all the tasks to be accomplished during the day...and this all before I even pick up my phone to see the stream of notifications and emails demanding my attention. My day isn't meant to start like this and neither is yours! Our **ALPHA** God created the day and we should wake and acknowledge the brand new mercies He gives and rejoice in His gracious giving of another day.

Does God exist before anything else in your day?

I begin my day with the Proverbs 31 Ministries First 5 App and I encourage you to download it today and give God your first, **ALPHA**, thoughts of the day.

2-29-20 Saturday

DAY 2: He is God ALMIGHTY

*"When Abram was 99 years old, the **Lord** appeared to him, saying, "I am **God Almighty**. Live in My presence and be blameless." Genesis 17:1 HCSB*

"God Almighty" or *"El Shaddai"* is used 7 times in the Old Testament and speaks to the Truth of God's mighty power over all things. He is God of *all* things. His power is limitless! In the context of Genesis 17:1, God was stating His power and authority over Abram and Sarai's lives through His covenant promise for Sarai to give birth to a child even though she was elderly and barren!

While pouring a blessing out over his children, Jacob said to Joseph:

*"by the God of your father who helps you, and by the **Almighty** who blesses you with blessings of the heavens above, blessings of the deep that lies below, and blessings of the breasts and the womb." Genesis 49:25 HCSB*

This **A**lmighty God is the God who gives us every breath we take and every new morning! He is the God of all blessings and every blessing comes from Him {James 1:17}.

He is *God Almighty* and deserving of our awe and wonder, praise and recognition as *Alpha* over every moment of our day!

Let's Get Real!

How can you make Almighty God your Alpha God today?

_____

_____

How will you place Him at the beginning of all things?

_____

_____

Can you think of any other characteristics of God beginning with "A"?

_____

_____

DAY 3: God is BEAUTIFUL!

*"One thing I have asked from the **Lord**, that I shall seek:*

*That I may dwell in the house of the **Lord** all the days of my life,*

*To behold the beauty of the **Lord***

And to meditate in His temple." Psalm 27:4

What is **beauty**?

When I started digging into the original language of the *"Beauty of the Lord"* I discovered in this verse it means: **Delightfulness, Pleasantness, Favor.**

This word comes from the Hebrew word *na'em* which is: agreeableness, i.e. Delight, suitableness, splendor or grace — beauty, pleasant(-ness).

"On that day the LORD of Hosts will become a crown of beauty and a diadem of splendor to the remnant of His people" Isaiah 28:5 HCSB

The Hebrew word for *beauty* in this verse is: **beauty, honor, glory.**

"Your eyes will see the King in His beauty..." Isaiah 33:17 HCSB

The Hebrew here means *absolute* and *ideal beauty!*

So with all these words associated with the *Beauty of the Lord*...what does it mean?

I love this definition from John Piper[1]:

> *"So here is an attempt at a definition. The glory of God is the infinite **beauty** and greatness of God's manifold perfections. The infinite **beauty** — and I am focusing on the manifestation of his character and his worth and his attributes, all of his perfections and greatness are **beautiful** as they are seen and there are many of them. That is why I use the word manifold."*

God's character and all of His attributes are **beautiful**. His definition of **beauty** is internal...it is what lies within His very nature and being. His glory, honor, grace, favor...everything we are studying in the A to Z of God's Character are what make Him **beautiful.**

God's character is absolute and ideal *beauty!*

That certainly gives me hope!

We know the Lord said to Samuel, *"Do not look on his appearance or on the height of his stature, because I have rejected him. For the **Lord** sees not as man sees: man looks on the outward*

*appearance, but the **Lord** looks on the heart."* 1 Samuel 16:7
ESV and it is your heart and Christ in it where true *beauty* lies.

We are made in the image of God. We were made to reflect His ***beauty*** through our salvation in Christ and the Holy Spirit living inside us. Absolute and ideal *beauty* is improved not from a bottle of foundation or clothing, but in becoming more and more like Christ every day.

We become more ***beautiful*** as we understand who God is and the person He created us to be.

We become more ***beautiful*** when we embrace the true beauty God has placed inside each one of us...a longing for Himself.

"Do not be conformed to this age, but be transformed by the renewing of your mind, so that you may discern what is the good, pleasing, and perfect will of God." Romans 12:2 HCSB

Let's Get Real!

How does God's definition help to shape your thoughts toward beauty?

_____

_____

How can you reflect the Beauty of the Lord today?

_____

_____

Can you think of any other characteristics of God beginning with "B"?

_____

_____

[1] http://www.gotquestions.org/Bible-beauty.html

3-5-20

DAY 4: God is COMPASSIONATE!

Merriam Webster defines *"Compassion"* as:

sympathetic consciousness of others' distress together with a desire to alleviate it

Compassion is the desire to come to the rescue. It is the desire to bring relief.

Exodus 34:6 shows God's *compassion* is rooted in love:

"The Lord passed by before him and proclaimed: "The Lord, the Lord, the compassionate and gracious God, slow to anger, and abounding in loyal love and faithfulness" Exodus 34:6 NET

Many times in the Old Testament *compassion* is paired with forgiveness and grace.

I had so much fun looking up the original Hebrew for *compassion!*

Strongs 7349: *"rachum"* is always used of God and speaks to Him being *compassionate* and *merciful*

"They refused to listen, And did not remember Your wondrous

deeds which You had performed among them; So they became stubborn and appointed a leader to return to their slavery in Egypt. But You are a God of forgiveness, Gracious and compassionate, Slow to anger and abounding in lovingkindness; And You did not forsake them." Nehemiah 9:17 NASB

Strongs 7356: *"racham"* again speaks of God's *compassion* and *mercy.*

"Nothing set apart for destruction is to remain in your hand, so that the Lord *will turn from His burning anger and grant you mercy, show you compassion, and multiply you as He swore to your fathers." Deuteronomy 13:17 HCSB*

Strongs 7355: *"racham"* tells of God's *compassion* founded in *love.*

"But the Lord was gracious to them and had compassion on them and turned to them because of His covenant with Abraham, Isaac, and Jacob, and would not destroy them or cast them from His presence until now." 2 Kings 13:23 NASB

"'For the mountains may be removed and the hills may shake, But My lovingkindness will not be removed from you, And My covenant of peace will not be shaken,' Says the Lord who has compassion on you." Isaiah 54:10 NASB

This is not the exhaustive list of Hebrew words translated into *compassion* but it is enough to show: God's *compassion* is His mercy.

Rooted in His love for us, His created children, God's *compassion* is His decision to spare us from the consequences of our actions and decisions.

God's *compassion* preserved His covenant promise: *"but the Lord was gracious to them, had compassion on them, and turned toward them because of His covenant with Abraham, Isaac, and Jacob. He was not willing to destroy them. Even now He has not banished them from His presence." 2 Kings 13:23 HCSB*

God's *compassionate* heart showers mercies upon us every day giving us life. He looks upon His redeemed children with love and pity. It is because of His *compassion* that we can receive forgiveness and be freed from the consequences of our actions that we rightly deserve.

One thing I discovered I love is the comparison between the *compassion* of God we see in the Old Testament, and the *compassion* of Christ we see in the New Testament. Jesus is God the Son, however; He is also fully human and in Him, we see human *compassion* in action!

Through the Gospels {Matthew, Mark, Luke, and John}, we see the Greek word *"σπλαγχνίζομαι (splagchnizomai)"* used to describe Jesus' *compassion.* It is a sense of being moved from the very core of your being to have pity, show *compassion* from the *"seat of the affections"* of your being.

Jesus' *compassion* caused Him to:

- heal the sick {Matthew 14:14, Mark 1:41},

- feed the hungry {Matthew 15:32, Mark 8:2},

- forgive debt and sin {Matthew 18:27-35},

- give sight to the blind {Matthew 20:34},

- teach the crowds {Mark 6:34},

- cast out demons {Mark 9:22} and

- comfort the mourning {Luke 7:13}.

His parables speak of *compassion* being a "Good Samaritan" to those in need {Luke 10:33, 36-37} and forgiving and welcoming, with open arms, the prodigals in your life whether family or friends {Luke 15:20-24}.

Jesus' *compassion* was the foundation for sending out laborers into His harvest:

*"When He saw the crowds, He felt **compassion** for them, because they were weary and worn out, like sheep without a shepherd. Then He said to His disciples, 'The harvest is abundant, but the workers are few. Therefore, pray to the Lord of the harvest to send out workers into His harvest.'" Matthew 9:36-38 HCSB*

We are called to reflect the mercy of God and be moved by the **compassion** of Christ to show love, share the Gospel, and help bring in His harvest.

DAY 5: CREATOR God!

"In the beginning God created the heavens and the earth." Genesis 1:1 HCSB

He is the ***creator*** of ALL things! He shaped the whole earth! He spoke creation into existence!

In 2009 I was teaching in a small Christian School in Dundee, Scotland when it closed down due to lack of students/income. Application after application led to a dead-end. I felt so lost and confused over my future. I knew my limited savings would soon run out leaving me with no means to pay the dreaded mortgage!

I also knew I needed to spend time listening to the Lord and not to everyone around me, so I packed up my tent and my parent's dog and escaped to the country!

For three days I sat in my tent with a dog, Bible, and notebook as my tangible companions and the Lord as my guide. I drove around the beautiful countryside. I read, wrote, prayed, and sat in silence with ***creation's*** song as my entertainment. As I drove along a road on the third day, I felt the Lord prompting me to stop and walk to the top of a mountain. It was a tough climb but I knew He had something for me at the top so I kept on climbing!

Once I reached the top of that mountain the splendor of the Lord was on display all around me. I looked out over mountains to the East and to the West, across the ocean to the Isle of Lewis where He had brought great revival years ago.

"Do you not know? Have you not heard? The Everlasting God, the LORD, the Creator of the ends of the earth Does not become weary or tired. His understanding is inscrutable. He gives strength to the weary, And to him who lacks might He increases power. Though youths grow weary and tired, And vigorous young men stumble badly, Yet those who wait for the LORD Will gain new strength; They will mount up with wings like eagles, They will run and not get tired, They will walk and not become weary." Isaiah 40:28-31 NASB

I knew in an instant that the **Creator God**, author of all creation, author of my life, had a plan! He comforted me with the knowledge that, if He could create all the beauty and splendor that lay before me, He could create beauty in my life and I could trust Him to show me His plan.

"Your eyes saw me when I was inside the womb. All the days ordained for me were recorded in your scroll before one of them came into existence." Psalm 139:16 NET

"By faith we understand that the universe was created by God's command, so that what is seen has been made from things that are not visible." Hebrews 11:3 HCSB

"But we know that there is only one God, the Father, who created everything, and we live for him. And there is only one Lord, Jesus Christ, through whom God made everything and through whom we have been given life." 1 Corinthians 8:6 NLT

One of our ***created*** purposes is to show compassion!

"Worthy are You, our Lord and our God, to receive glory and honor and power; for You created all things, and because of Your will they existed, and were created." Revelation 4:11 NASB

Let's Get Real!

Where is your favorite place to see God's creation on display?

_____

_____

Do you trust the Creator God to create something beautiful in your life?

_____

_____

How can you show compassion to the world around you today?

_____

_____

Can you think of any other characteristics of God beginning with "C"?

_____

_____

DAY 6: God is DIVINE!

"For His invisible attributes, that is, His eternal power and divine nature, have been clearly seen since the creation of the world, being understood through what He has made." Romans 1:20 HCSB

"His divine power has given us everything required for life and godliness through the knowledge of Him who called us by His own glory and goodness. By these He has given us very great and precious promises, so that through them you may share in the divine nature, escaping the corruption that is in the world because of evil desires." 2 Peter 1:3-4 HCSB

The Greek word we get ***"Divine"*** from is *"theios"* and simply means "manifesting the characteristics of God's nature" — to think of God as *divine* is to consider all of His attributes and characteristics. "Theios" comes from "theos" which is to consider God as *Godhead.* He is the head of the whole universe.

To consider God as *divine* is to recognize His supreme power and authority over all things.

He is in control, He sees everything and is at work in everything and because He is our *divine* God: *"We know that all things work together for the good of those who love God: those who are called according to His purpose." Romans 8:28 HCSB*

As we continue on our journey through the A to Z of God's Character and unveil more of His characteristics, we will grasp a deeper sense of His *divine* nature!

DAY 7: God is our DELIVERER!

"The Lord is my rock, my fortress, and my deliverer" 2 Samuel 22:2 HCSB

When I think of a ***deliverer*** I think of the mailman bringing me something — and it's not normally anything good! So what does it mean to say that God, in very nature, is a *deliverer*? What is He delivering?

The Hebrew word *"palat"* gives us some insight. God, the deliverer, is the one who will help you escape and bring you into safety and security. He is ***delivering*** you.

2 Samuel 22 is a song David proclaimed on the day He was *delivered* into safety from his enemies.

God is the only One with the *divine* authority to *deliver* us from all we face in this world.

"I am afflicted and needy; the Lord thinks of me. You are my helper and my deliverer; my God, do not delay." Psalm 40:17 HCSB

God, who has *divine* authority over all things, has the power and ability to work in your life and circumstances in order to orchestrate events and people to do His will and work. This may not look like you think it should at times! But we can be sure that He is working for good and His purpose.

Jesus is the ultimate *deliverer* rescuing us from our sin and consequences when He died on the cross. Jesus took all the pain and punishment for all the wrong I have done. He suffered in my place so that my *Deliverer God* could work good in all things and rescue me from my sin. One day He will *deliver* me to the ultimate place of security in Heaven.

When it seems like you are not in a place of security — remember your eternal security in Heaven. Remember God is working. I can see times in my life when I have suffered {not even 1% of what Christ endured} and it has been for the purpose of someone else being *delivered* from what they were facing.

Let's Get Real!

What other characteristics can you think of beginning with D?

_____

_____

How does it comfort you to think of God as *Divine* over all things?

———————————————

———————————————

Can you think of times in your life when God has been your *Deliverer?*

———————————————

———————————————

Can you think of any other characteristics of God beginning with "D"?

———————————————

———————————————

DAY 8: God is ETERNAL...EVERLASTING!

"Now to the King eternal, immortal, invisible, the only God, be honor and glory forever and ever. Amen." 1 Timothy 1:17 HCSB

God is *eternal.* He is ageless and forever. He was and is and is to come {Revelation 1:8}. He is *alpha* and *omega!*

"Before the mountains were born Or You gave birth to the earth and the world, Even from everlasting to everlasting, You are God." Psalm 90:2 NASB

The Hebrew for **everlasting** means quite simply forever, continually existing. I will admit I have used this word in extremes...it didn't really feel like it took *forever* to hear back about that job, or those test results, or the server to bring our meal.

Comparative to the eternality of God...our lives are a mere blip on the radar!

Comparative to our eternity in Heaven...our struggles are a mere blip on the radar.

"For momentary, light affliction is producing for us an eternal weight of glory far beyond all comparison" 2 Corinthians 4:17 NASB

Everlasting in terms of God's nature and words means exactly that — never-ending, forever, without end, *eternal.* So when we read about His *"everlasting covenant"* with His people we can take Him at His Word! He is not being extreme — He is being real! There is also no end to the awesomeness of His nature and characteristics!

"When the bow is in the cloud, then I will look upon it, to remember the everlasting covenant between God and every living creature of all flesh that is on the earth." Genesis 9:16 NASB

Let's Get Real!

Are you like me — have you used "forever" to describe momentary blips?! I challenge you as I challenge myself to stop being extreme and be real!

How does it comfort you knowing that God's promises to us are *everlasting?*

_____

_____

What other characteristics of God can you think of beginning with E?

_____

_____

DAY 9: God is FAITHFUL and FORGIVING!

"If we are faithless, He remains faithful, for He cannot deny Himself." 2 Timothy 2:13 NASB

The Greek word here for faithful is *"pistos"* and means trustworthy and believing. The *faithfulness* of God denotes a loyalty. He is true, sure, and loyal to His Word.

2 Timothy 2:13 means that when we refuse to believe and trust in the Lord, and fail to put our faith in Him ... He maintains His position as our **Faithful**, Trustworthy God because He is not able to be false and uncharacteristic to who He is!

> *Even when I cannot understand circumstances in my life...God is **faithful** and I can trust that His ways and thoughts are far superior to my own! Isaiah 55:9*

> *When I feel like He has abandoned me...He is faithful to His promise to protect me from all evil. {Psalm 121:7}*

> *When I doubt my life has purpose...I can believe in my **Faithful God** who created me with a purpose and plan in mind!*

"For we are His workmanship, created in Christ Jesus for good works, which God prepared beforehand so that we would walk in them." Ephesians 2:10 NASB

So whatever you are doubting or not believing God for today take comfort in the truth that He remains *faithful* to His call over your life and turn back to His promises knowing that He is unable to deny them!

God will remain **faithful**, true, loyal, and trustworthy to His call over your life!

"If we confess our sins, He is faithful and righteous to forgive us our sins and to cleanse us from all unrighteousness." 1 John 1:9 HCSB

Forgiveness: release, let go, lay aside — God releases us from our sins and lays them aside. They are no longer attached to us. We are freed from the penalty of our sin when we are *forgiven* by our Father God!

One of my favorite illustrations of a father's *forgiveness* in Scripture is Jesus' parable of The Prodigal Son {Luke 15:11-31}.

The son took his inheritance, half of his father's estate, and ran away. Having squandered it, he found himself in a pit...with pigs! I love how the HCSB describes his turning point: *"When he came to his senses..." v 17.* The son went home willing to be a servant in his father's household as he believed he was unworthy of being called his son.

Oh how I can relate to the prodigal son. I believed my sin was beyond **forgiveness** and I was unworthy of acceptance and redemption. These next verses describe the *forgiveness* our Father God extends to us:

"But while the son was still a long way off, his father saw him and was filled with compassion. He ran, threw his arms around his neck, and kissed him..."But the father told his slaves, 'Quick! Bring out the best robe and put it on him; put a ring on his finger and sandals on his feet. Then bring the fattened calf and slaughter it, and let's celebrate with a feast, because this son of mine was dead and is alive again; he was lost and is found!' So they began to celebrate." v 20, 22-24

The *forgiveness* of the Father looks beyond our past decisions and deserved consequences!

When we turn to our Father God He is overcome with love and compassion and rejoices over us *coming to our senses* and running home into His arms!

God is *faithful* to His promise to *forgive!*

Jesus reflected the *forgiveness* of His Father and demonstrated His authority as the Son while He was dying on the cross. Speaking of the very people punishing and crucifying Him, He said: *"Father, forgive them, because they do not know what they are doing." Luke 23:34 HCSB*

Let's Get Real!

Have you doubted the *faithfulness* of God through your thoughts or attitude?

_____

_____

Admit your doubt to Him right now! Come to Him believing in His *faithfulness* over His plan for your life.

_____

_____

Have you experienced the true *forgiveness* our Father God extends to us with open arms? Please reach out to me on Social Media at @srhtrvs12 if you need more information.

_____

_____

What other characteristics of God can you think of beginning with F?

_____

_____

DAY 10: God is GRACIOUS!

"The Lord is gracious and compassionate, slow to anger and great in faithful love." Psalm 145:8 HCSB

The Hebrew for *gracious* in this verse is *"channun"* and used to describe the Lord alone. More often than not it is paired with *compassion,* which we studied a few days ago. God is the *only* One who can show true compassion and **grace** to His people.

Another Hebrew word coming from the same root word as *"channun"* is *"chanan"* which, when used in reference to God, speaks about Him granting redemption and *deliverance* from our enemies and from our sins.

"Therefore the Lord longs to be gracious to you, And therefore He waits on high to have compassion on you." Isaiah 30:18 NASB

In his book *"Bible Doctrine"* Wayne Grudem[1] simply defines *grace* as

"God's goodness toward those who deserve only punishment."

The beauty is it is part of God's character to be *gracious* and because He is unchanging {James 1:17} His *grace* is always available. God's *grace* is not dependent on what we have done or who we are. It is not ranked by our position at work or in church. His *grace* is not given in greater amounts to those who are involved in 10 ministries, over those struggling just to make it through the doors of church. God's *grace* comes from a place of His love and compassion for His children.

God's *gracious* character ultimately caused Him to send His Son to give us what we do not deserve...salvation and deliverance from our sins. He longs so much to be *gracious* and compassionate toward us, that He offered up His own Son to take the penalty for all of our sins so that we can have eternal life with Him in Heaven.

I love this description of the *grace* of our Lord Jesus Christ found in the HELPS word study:

"is preeminently used of the Lord's favor – freely extended to give Himself away to people (because He is 'always leaning toward them')."

"We have redemption in Him through His blood, the forgiveness of our trespasses, according to the riches of His grace that He lavished on us with all wisdom and understanding." Ephesians 1:7-8 HCSB

"For you are saved by grace through faith, and this is not from yourselves; it is God's gift — not from works, so that no one can boast." Ephesians 2:8-9 HCSB

God, through His Son Jesus, showers His *grace* upon us every day by giving us deliverance from the consequences of our sins. There is nothing we can do to earn God's *grace* as it is a gift! Because of His love and compassion toward His children, He freely lavishes us with *grace...His goodness...*when we deserve nothing but punishment.

So often I hear people use the expression *"it is only by the **grace** of God I...".* That sentence can be finished in so many ways very personal to each one of us but the truth remains: yes...it *is* only by the *grace...goodness...compassion...love* of God that we are....

I am sure you all have a story to tell and I would love to hear how the *grace* of God has delivered you. I became a Christian at the age of 13 by recognizing my need for Jesus to be my Savior, but I did not make Him Lord of my life...I let the world take care of that. God **graced** me through my late teens and early twenties. He **graced** me through situations my sinful nature found me in. He **graced** me back into the company of Christian friends and eventually to realizing I needed to make Him Lord and walk away from my past. It is by His *grace* I survived those years and live now to serve Him.

Let's Get Real!

How has the *grace* of the Lord been evident in your life?

_____

_____

Remember, we are made to reflect the characteristics of God...who can you extend *grace* to today?

_____

_____

What other characteristics of God can you think of beginning with G?

_____

_____

[1] http://www.waynegrudem.com/bible-doctrine/

DAY 11: God is Holy, Holy, Holy!

"Holy, Holy, Holy, is the Lord of hosts,
The whole earth is full of His glory." Isaiah 6:3 NASB

"Holy, holy, holy is the Lord God, the Almighty, who was and who
is and who is to come." Revelation 4:8 NASB

The word *Holy* is used many times in Scripture; however, this trifold expression *"Holy, Holy, Holy"* is only used these two times. It was a Jewish custom to repeat a word multiple times for emphasis ~ "land, land, land" {Jeremiah 22:29}, "ruin, ruin, ruin" {Ezekiel 21:27}. So when the prophet Isaiah and John both had visions from the Lord including angels around the throne of God calling out *"Holy, Holy, Holy"* they are passionately emphasizing the true holiness of God while in His presence.

I believe the trifold expression also represents the *Holy Trinity* — God the Father, Jesus the Son, and the Holy Spirit all possess this *holiness.*

"Holy" = *"qadosh"*

God is Sacred

God is Set Apart

God is Separate from Sin

God is Exalted

"Holiness is an attribute of God that distinguishes Himself and His creation." Don Stewart

God's *holiness* is what separates Him from all creation and makes Him distinct. His *holiness* is not an attribute we naturally posses...it can only be possessed through Christ.

In the Old Testament construction of the tabernacle they were instructed to build a "Holy Place" dedicated to the Lord's service. They were then to hang a veil which:

"will make a division for you between the Holy Place and the Most Holy Place." Exodus 26:33 NET

The *Most Holy Place* was where the Ark of the Covenant containing the stone tablet, on which the 10 Commandments were written, was held. Once a year, the chief priest would enter in order to make atonement for the sins of all the people. There were many rules and regulations Aaron had to follow when he went beyond the veil into the *Most Holy Place {Leviticus 16}*. If these rules were not followed then Aaron risked death {Leviticus 16:2}.

God is so Holy, our sinful nature cannot survive in His presence.

God is so Holy, a veil separated Him from His people.

Hear this though...that was Old Testament...old covenant! It is so crucial to understand these things even though we are under a new covenant because they help us fully understand and appreciate in awe, the power of Christ and all He has done for us.

At the moment of His death upon the cross THIS happened...

"And behold, the veil of the temple was torn in two from top to bottom; and the earth shook and the rocks were split." Matthew 27:51 NASB

Jesus' death on the cross removed the separation between God and His people. Jesus is *the* High Priest who entered into *the* Holy Place of Heaven to appear before the Father and make atonement for all of our sins once and for all!

"For the Messiah did not enter a sanctuary made with hands (only a model of the true one) but into heaven itself, so that He might now appear in the presence of God for us. He did not do this to offer Himself many times, as the high priest enters the sanctuary yearly with the blood of another. Otherwise, He would have had to suffer many times since the foundation of the world. But now He has appeared one time, at the end of the ages, for the removal of sin by the sacrifice of Himself." Hebrews 9:24-26 HCSB

Jesus is our High Priest granting us access to our *Holy, Holy, Holy God* and sits at the right hand of His Father interceding for us continually.

> *"Who is the one who condemns?*
> *Christ Jesus is the One who died,*
> *but even more, has been raised;*
> *He also is at the right hand of God*
> *and intercedes for us." Romans 8:34 HCSB*

We have forgiveness, but we also have a responsibility to honor and value that gift. When you receive the most precious gift – you want to protect it, you want to use it as it was intended and not take it for granted or be unappreciative.

Our forgiveness is a gift from our *Holy* God and we are called to cherish it by living our lives as He intended.

> *"But as the One who called you is holy, you also are to be holy in all your conduct; for it is written, Be holy, because I am holy." 1 Peter 1:15-16 HCSB*

Let's Get Real!

How does it make you feel knowing we do not have to live under the Old Covenant with a veil separating us from our Holy God?

Aaron could only access the Most Holy Place once a year on behalf of the people. We now have 24/7 access to our Holy, Holy, Holy God through Jesus — do you use that access?

What other characteristics of God can you think of beginning with H?

DAY 12: God is INCOMPREHENSIBLE!

That's a pretty big word for a simple thought — **we just don't** *get* **God at times!**

How many times have you cried out to the Lord begging to understand a situation?

How many times have you wondered why He allows suffering in the world?

Do you sometimes question His purpose...or your purpose?

The fact of the matter is — we will *never* fully understand God — He is *incomprehensible!*

"Great is the Lord, and highly to be praised,
And His greatness is unsearchable." Psalm 145:3 NASB

It is impossible to completely comprehend the greatness of God!

Great is our Lord, and abundant in power; his understanding is beyond measure." Psalm 147:5 ESV

There is no end to the understanding of our Father God and so we cannot possibly comprehend the way He understands all things. Our inability to fully comprehend the Lord is not a new thing! In the Old Testament David admits he cannot possibly understand: *"This extraordinary knowledge is beyond me. It is lofty; I am unable to reach it."* *Psalm 139:6 HCSB.* God's knowledge is *incomprehensible!*

I love the simplicity of Paul:

"Oh, the depth of the riches both of the wisdom and the knowledge of God! How unsearchable His judgments and untraceable His ways!" Romans 11:33 HCSB

and again in 1 Corinthians 2:11 HCSB when he says: "no one knows the thoughts of God except the Spirit of God."

How far removed are we from understand the mind, knowledge, love, ways of God...? How far away are the heavens?

"'For My thoughts are not your thoughts,
and your ways are not My ways.'
This is the Lord's declaration.
'For as heaven is higher than earth,
so My ways are higher than your ways,
and My thoughts than your thoughts.'" Isaiah 55:8-9 HCSB

Don't lose heart about God being *incomprehensible*...it just means there is always something to learn!

My personal thoughts on our God being *incomprehensible* are this...we could not handle the truth! Our human minds are not equipped to hold full understanding of all God's ways and if we did, it would remove the mystery. In His *grace,* God withholds full knowledge from us so that we are not burdened with explaining such mysteries to others who, without the Holy Spirit, have even less chance of understanding God.

Instead of striving to obtain full understanding...which is impossible...we live by faith! *"For we walk by faith, not by sight"* 2 *Corinthians 5:7 HCSB* and so we can believe *all* God says and does because:

> *"the word of the Lord is right, and all His work is trustworthy." Psalm 33:4 HCSB*

So when I fail to understand a situation I can trust that God does and He is right.

When I struggle looking around at the suffering I can trust God sees and is at work because He is right.

When I doubt the purpose for my life I can trust God's right plan!

> God is *incomprehensible* but He fully comprehends all things...including me!

Let's Get Real!

Is there a particular are you are struggling to understand and allowing it to consume your thoughts? Pray over it. Lay it at the foot of the cross and hand it to our fully comprehending God with faith that He is right and at work.

_____

_____

Do not lose heart over the incomprehensibility of God! Remember there is always something to learn so keep reading and growing in your knowledge of what He wants to teach you today.

_____

_____

What other characteristics of God can you think of beginning with I?

_____

_____

DAY 13: God is JEALOUS … over you!

"For you must not worship any other god, for the Lord, whose name is Jealous, is a jealous God." Exodus 34:14 NET

The original Hebrew word used in this verse is אֵל קַנָּא – Qanna and is only used 6 times in Scripture — always in reference to God. In Exodus 34:14, God doesn't simply name *jealousy* as a character trait, but He actually names Himself *Jealous.* He doesn't only act with *jealousy — He is Jealous!*

The Lord speaks these words to Moses on Mount Sinai when He reaffirms His covenant with him. All the people had begun to doubt in the Lord and in Moses' leadership, and so had built for themselves golden calf to worship and sacrifice to {Exodus 32:1-6}.

God's *jealousy* rose within Him as He saw the people He had created and rescued from slavery in Egypt go against His first commandment: *"You shall have no other gods before Me." Exodus 20:3 NASB.* Moses pleaded with the Lord to show mercy to the people.

Many were destroyed and those who had been involved in the

sin of idolatry were blotted out of the Lord's book. He was so enraged that He instructed Moses to move the people but He would not be with them lest He consume them! He did continue to appear to Moses and instruct him on how to lead the people, and Moses continued to plead for mercy on behalf of the people {Exodus 33}.

So then we arrive in Exodus 34 and the renewal of the covenant and God again writes the Ten Commandments on tablets of stone {the originals had been broken –Exodus 32:19}. He reminds Moses of many of His other characteristics: His *mercy, grace, love, faithfulness, and **forgiving** nature.* This reaffirmation of His covenant and commandments came with an order to *"tear down their altars and smash their sacred pillars and cut down their Asherim {sacred poles for worship}" Exodus 34:13 NASB*

> *Our* jealous *God commands us to worship Him, and Him alone.*
>
> *God is* jealous *when the praise and recognition due to Him is given to idol.*
>
> *God is rightly* jealous *when His command to worship Him alone is broken.*

We belong to God alone. He created us. We are His. God is the only One who is perfect and has the power to forgive sin, and so His *jealous* nature is perfect in motive and response.

There is someone who longs for your undivided attention, every thought and love...God is *jealous* for you! He first created you in His mind and loved you so much that He couldn't do anything other than bring you into existence. We were created and commanded to worship Him and so when do anything else...He is *jealous!*

We are programmed to view **jealousy** as a negative trait and in human terms it is! When we hear the word *jealous* our minds run to the feelings of envy leading to rivalry and bitter thought. However, there is such a thing as Godly *jealousy.*

"For I am jealous for you with a godly jealousy; for I betrothed you to one husband, so that to Christ I might present you as a pure virgin." 2 Corinthians 11:2 NASB

Paul was so passionate about the salvation of the people of the church of Corinth that he described his desire to belong to Christ alone as *jealousy.* He didn't want the people to be influenced by and snatched away, in thought or deed, by the deception and false teaching.

"But I am afraid that, as the serpent deceived Eve by his craftiness, your minds will be led astray from the simplicity and purity of devotion to Christ. For if one comes and preaches another Jesus whom we have not preached, or you receive a different spirit which you have not received, or a different gospel which you have not accepted, you bear this beautifully." 2 Corinthians 11:3-4 NASB

Godly jealousy *is when our hearts are stirred to action in the Spiritual battle over souls.*

Let's Get Real!

How does it make you feel to think of God being jealous over you? How can you respond to God's jealousy over you today?

_____

_____

Is there something or someone you are placing before Him? Have you made an idol for yourself in placing too much importance in a person, job, situation...? Confess your idolatry to the Lord today and place Him first in your life.

_____

_____

Can you think of any other characteristics of God beginning with J?

_____

_____

DAY 14: God is KING of KINGS!

Growing up in Scotland I have been very aware of the idea of a Monarch, King, Queen, Princes, and Princesses all of my life! I may or may not have dreamed of marrying Prince William and becoming a real princess!

Although not something we did, I grew up knowing about the nation-wide tradition of families gathering around the television at 3pm on Christmas Day to hear the "Queen's Speech" — to many, she became one of the main focal points of their Christmas Day.

I had a different monarch as the focal point of my day.

King Jesus!

The British monarch is Head of the Armed Forces.

My King of Kings is the Head of Angel Armies!

"Who is this King-Glory? God-of-the-Angel-Armies: he is King-Glory." Psalm 24:10 MSG

The British monarch is the Fount of Justice but no longer administers the law.

My King of Kings is the Just Justifier who has all authority!

"The Lord has established His throne in heaven, and His kingdom

rules over all." Psalm 103:19 HCSB

"He would be just and the justifier of the one who has faith in Jesus." Romans 3:26 NASB

The British monarch is a sinner whose days on earth are numbered and so the monarch is continually changing — passing from flawed human to flawed human and influenced by changing times and culture.

My King of Kings is the only King of Heaven!

"Your kingdom is an everlasting kingdom; Your rule is for all generations." Psalm 145:13 HCSB

"This is what the Lord, the King of Israel and its Redeemer, the Lord of Hosts, says: I am the first and I am the last. There is no God but Me." Isaiah 44:6 HCSB

Jesus, as the Son of God, is the King of Kings and the Lord of Lords!

"My kingdom is not of this world," said Jesus. "If My kingdom were of this world, My servants would fight, so that I wouldn't be handed over to the Jews. As it is, My kingdom does not have its origin here." "You are a king then?" Pilate asked. "You say that I'm a king," Jesus replied. "I was born for this, and I have come into the world for this: to testify to the truth. Everyone who is of the

truth listens to My voice." John 18:36-37 HCSB

"And He has a name written on His robe and on His thigh: KING OF KINGS AND LORD OF LORDS." Revelation 19:16 HCSB

"Now to the King eternal, immortal, invisible, the only God, be honor and glory forever and ever. Amen." 1 Timothy 1:17 HCSB

Let's Get Real!

How does it make you feel to think of God being King? Do you respect Him as the authoritative forever-reigning monarch over your life?

_____

_____

God commands His angel armies to protect you? Thank Him today for being Head of that Army!

_____

_____

What other characteristics of God can you think of beginning with K?

_____

_____

DAY 15: God is LOVE so gives us Himself!

"Dear friends, let us love *one another, because* love *is from God, and everyone who loves has been born of God and knows God. The one who does not love does not know God, because God is* love. *God's* love *was revealed among us in this way: God sent His One and Only Son into the world so that we might live through Him.* **Love** *consists in this: not that we* **loved** *God, but that He* **loved** *us and sent His Son to be the propitiation for our sins." 1 John 4:7-10 HCSB*

God *is love* **and so God gives Himself when He** *loves* **us.**

In 1 John 4:8 *"God is love"* the original language states *"God's nature is summed up in love"* meaning that everything God is extends from *love.* **Love** is not an affection God decides to show at certain times or to certain people — it is the very essence of who He is!

His *love* never fails: *"He loves righteousness and justice; the earth is full of the Lord's unfailing love." Psalm 33:5 HCSB*

His *love* endures forever: *"Give thanks to the Lord, for He is good. His love is eternal..." Psalm 136 HCSB*

His *love* causes Him to give Himself to all — unconditionally.

"For God loved the world in this way: He gave His One and Only Son, so that everyone who believes in Him will not perish but have eternal life. For God did not send His Son into the world that He might condemn the world, but that the world might be saved through Him." John 3:16-17 HCSB

So what is our response to God's *love?*

Our first response to God's *love* is to accept it.

We have to accept His *love* into our hearts by recognizing true *love* only exists from and through Him. His *unconditional love* caused God to send His Son Jesus into the world to pay the price and penalty for all the sins you and I have ever committed and will commit in the future. Jesus died a sinners death on the cross and took upon Himself the weight of the world, including separation from His Father in Heaven for one purpose — you.

Jesus obeyed His Father's command to die for you and me so that we never have to face the harsh reality of the punishment we deserve for every time we sin against our Creator. Our response to this display of *love* is to, first admit we are a sinner {Romans 3:23}, then believe that God, in His grace and mercy, freely releases us from our punishment into eternal life {Romans 6:23}. Lastly, our response to this display of God's *love* on the cross is this, we call upon the Name of the Lord {Romans 10:13}, confess our sins, and believe in the power of the resurrection giving us a new life {Romans 10:9-10}...then live out that believe in our lives....

Our second response to God's *love* is to show *love*.

"He said to him, "Love the Lord your God with all your heart, with all your soul, and with all your mind. This is the greatest and most important command." Matthew 22:37-38 HCSB

Every time we fail to *love* the Lord in our day we are stepping further away from who He created and commanded us to be.

"Anyone who does not love does not know God, because God is love." 1 John 4:8

Just as I had to study my husband to understand who he is and what he *loves*, we have to study to understand who God is and what *love* is — and we do that by studying our Bibles.

The truth is...I do not *love* God or others all the time due to the way I think and act.

"But how can they call on Him they have not believed in? And how can they believe without hearing about Him?...So faith comes from what is heard, and what is heard comes through the message about Christ." Romans 10:14-17 HCSB

I believe *love* and trust go hand in hand. To believe in Christ in this verse is to entrust your life to Him.

The Greek word for "faith" is *"pistis"* and means to have belief, trust, confidence, fidelity, faithfulness in what we place our faith in.

Loving the Lord with everything means learning what He loves.

One of my favorite verses concerning the *love* of God is:

"For I am persuaded that not even death or life,

angels or rulers,

things present or things to come, hostile powers,

height or depth, or any other created thing

will have the power to separate us

from the love of God that is in Christ Jesus our Lord!" Romans

8:38-39 HCSB

Let's Get Real!

Have you responded to God's Love for you?

_____

_____

How can you show your love for God today?

_____

_____

There are so many incredible verses from Scripture discussing the LOVE of the Lord. What other verses can you find telling us how to show God's love to the world around us?

_____

_____

What other characteristics of God can you think of beginning with L?

_____

_____

Day 16: He is a Merciful God!

"And the Lord passed by before him, and proclaimed, The Lord, The Lord God, merciful and gracious, longsuffering, and abundant in goodness and truth" Exodus 34:6 KJV

"But You, O Lord, are a God merciful and gracious, Slow to anger and abundant in lovingkindness and truth." Psalm 86:15 NASB

The Hebrew word מוֹחַר *rachum* is always used to speak of the *compassion* and *mercy* of God, and is always paired with words such as *grace* and *forgiveness*. It comes from the Hebrew word רַחַם *racham* which is a verb meaning to show *love* and *compassion*. I just love how these characteristics of God are intertwined and all extending from a place of *love!* Love is not simply an emotion God feels toward us — it spurs Him to act with compassion, grace, and **mercy.**

So how does God's *love* cause Him to act with *mercy?*

God's *love* causes Him to extend *mercy* and withhold the judgment and consequences we deserve for all of our sins. When we put our trust in Christ we receive His *mercy,* which saves us from experiencing His wrath and instead we experience forgiveness and freedom. His *grace* then gives us all that we do not deserve — His Holy Spirit and eternal life in Heaven. *Grace* and *mercy* walk hand-in-hand with the *love* of God.

"But God, who is rich in mercy, because of His great love that He had for us, made us alive with the Messiah even though we were dead in trespasses. You are saved by grace! Together with Christ Jesus He also raised us up and seated us in the heavens" Ephesians 2:4-6 HCSB

*"God's **mercy** means God's goodness toward those in misery and distress." ~* Wayne Grudem, Bible Doctrine.[1]

Is there anything we can *do* to obtain God's *mercy*?

No! We receive God's ***mercy*** and grace because He loves us — no other reason and there is nothing we can do to earn it. We just have to come to Him.

*"For He tells Moses: I will show **mercy** to whom I will show **mercy**, and I will have compassion on whom I will have compassion. So then it does not depend on human will or effort but on God who shows **mercy**." Romans 9:15-16 HCSB*

So, even when I don't deserve *mercy* or even stop and think to approach my God — He chooses to grant me *mercy* despite myself!

Is there an end to His *mercy?*

No! I love the beauty of the Old Testament being brought to life in Jesus. In the Tabernacle built in the time of Moses, the Ark of the Covenant {10 Commandments} and the *mercy* seat were contained in the Most Holy Place, only accessed by the High Priest once a year in order to make atonement and receive forgiveness for all of the people. When Jesus died and the veil of separation between the people and the Most Holy Place was torn — He became our High Priest granting access to the *mercy* seat for all — all the time! That is why the writer to the Hebrews said:

"Therefore let us draw near with confidence to the throne of grace, so that we may receive mercy and find grace to help in time of need." Hebrews 4:16 NASB

Jesus is our High Priest granting 24/7 access to the *mercy* seat of His Father in Heaven!

"Because of the Lord's faithful love
we do not perish,
for His mercies never end.
They are new every morning;
great is Your faithfulness!" Lamentations 3:22-23 HCSB

Let's Get Real!

Spend some time reflecting on the difference between grace and mercy. Write out your own definition of each.

_____

_____

Write a prayer of thanks to God for His mercy in your life today.

_____

_____

What other characteristics of God can you think of beginning with M?

_____

_____

[1] http://www.waynegrudem.com/bible-doctrine/

DAY 17: God Names and ReNames

Names and name meanings are a *huge* deal in the Bible and Biblical times. Names weren't simply chosen for how they sound or for being quirky or trending! Names were given to people due to the meaning they held.

Many people still hold to this tradition while choosing their child's name. I like to think my parents did when they called me Sarah — meaning *Princess* in Hebrew!! Although I'm sure I've been more of a Diva than a Princess in my life!

The incredible truth about God is that He is a *Naming* God! He Names and Renames as part of who He is and the love and direction He extends to His people.

When God renames you it is a moment of definition — of His call and sovereignty over your life.

Our *naming* God chooses to rename as a defining moment between the old and the new — between the past and the future He has planned.

Abram became Abraham

"No longer shall your name be called Abram, But your name shall be Abraham; For I have made you the father of a multitude of nations." Genesis 17:5 NASB

At the renewal of the covenant, when Abram was ninety-nine, God again promised to make him a father of nations. Abram, *"exalted father"*, became Abraham, *"father of a multitude"*.

Sarai became Sarah

"Then God said to Abraham, "As for Sarai your wife, you shall not call her name Sarai, but Sarah shall be her name." Genesis 17:15 NASB

I love this particular moment from our *Naming God.* He is placing His stamp upon her life. He did not change the meaning of her name but as a symbol of the covenant and stating His purpose over her life, He renamed Sarai as Sarah, which is a different form of the name with the same meaning of *"princess"*.

How God renames you might not seem dramatic but it is a symbol of His plan and purpose for your life.

Jacob became Israel

This renaming took place twice. The first time was a private renaming between the Lord and Jacob after they had wrestled all night {Genesis 32:28} and the second time feels like more of a ceremonial event in which God also reaffirms His covenant to make Israel into a nation of people.

> *"God said to him, 'Your name is Jacob; You shall no longer be called Jacob, But Israel shall be your name.' Thus He called him Israel. God also said to him, 'I am God Almighty; Be fruitful and multiply; A nation and a company of nations shall come from you, And kings shall come forth from you.'" Genesis 35:10-11*
> *NASB*

His name was changed from Jacob, *"He takes by the heel– cheats"*, to Israel, *"He strives with God"*. Jacob spent the night wrestling with the Lord and was then blessed by Him, which brought Israel to a place of surrender and worship. Again, after his second renaming occurrence, Israel's response was to set up a pillar to mark the place, and worship the Lord with an offering.

Saul became Paul

Unlike Abram, Sarai, and Jacob there was not a singular moment when Saul was renamed as Paul. Saul had a dramatic encounter with the Lord on the road to Damascus {Acts 9:1-19}. Immediately after this experience of revelation Saul, who had been a persecutor and murderer of Christians, was proclaiming the Truth:

"and immediately he began to proclaim Jesus in the synagogues, saying, "He is the Son of God." All those hearing him continued to be amazed, and were saying, "Is this not he who in Jerusalem destroyed those who called on this name, and who had come here for the purpose of bringing them bound before the chief priests?" But Saul kept increasing in strength and confounding the Jews who lived at Damascus by proving that this Jesus is the Christ." Acts 9:20-22 NASB

The name Saul is used in the book of Acts until chapter 13 where Luke writes *"But Saul, who was also known as Paul"* {v9} and he is thereafter referred to as Paul as he continues his life as God's servant and missionary to the people.

Saul means *"prayed for"* which I believe to be very fitting! How often do we pray for the people in our lives who have yet to have the veil removed from their eyes to see Christ. Paul means *"humble"* and again is so reflective of Paul, who would become one of the greatest and humblest New Testament missionaries and writer of almost half of the New Testament. Although he was not regularly referred to as Paul immediately following his conversion, it was at this point he humbled himself and became an obedient servant of the Lord.

Our *Naming God* redefines and repurposes our lives when He renames us! He names you according to your future — not your past!

Let's Get Real!

If you are a Christian, saved by **Grace** through **Faith** in Christ, then you have been renamed by your Father God. Do you still use names for yourself associated with your past — or do you name yourself as the Lord names you?

_____

_____

Spend some time thinking about the names the Lord has for you — His chosen child. Replace the names that once defined you by the names God uses to define you.

_____

_____

What other characteristics of God can you think of beginning with N?

_____

_____

DAY 18: God is Omnipresent

As we learned when we studied the Beauty of the Lord —
*God's character is absolute and ideal beauty and we were made
to reflect His beauty through our salvation in Christ and the Holy
Spirit living inside us.*

There are some of His attributes we can possess, which are
called the *communicable* attributes. Then there are the attributes
belonging to God alone — His *incommunicable* attributes, which
include His **holiness,** which we have already studied. Today we are
going to look into some more of His *incommunicable* attributes
and examine His greatness!

God is OMNI!

The word omni comes from the Latin word omnis, which
means *all.* It is a prefix used to create compound words such as
the following *incommunicable* characteristics of God.

God is *Omnipresent*

Omni = *all*

Presence, *Latin praesens =* **here**

God is *all here!* He is *everywhere!* God is the same for everyone and so anyone can say He is *omnipresent* in their lives and so He is everywhere at all times.

*"God does not have size or spatial dimension, and is **present** at every point of space with his whole being, yet God acts differently in different places." ~ Wayne Grudem, Bible Doctrine*

"Where can I go to escape Your Spirit?
Where can I flee from Your presence?
If I go up to heaven, You are there;
if I make my bed in Sheol, You are there.
If I live at the eastern horizon
or settle at the western limits,
even there Your hand will lead me;
Your right hand will hold on to me." Psalm 139:7-10 HCSB

"Am I a God at hand, declares the Lord, and not a God far away? Can a man hide himself in secret places so that I cannot see him? declares the Lord. Do I not fill heaven and earth? declares the Lord." Jeremiah 23:23-24 ESV

God's *omnipresence* is both a comfort and a warning!

There is no place we can go from God's presence and so He sees everything! Yes, that means He sees and hears all the things I would rather He hadn't. We cannot close the door on God and keep Him out of a part of our lives. The other side of that incredible truth is that He *does* see everything. He is present in your weakness and trials. He is beside you as you walk through pain and suffering.

When I was going through a time of uncertainty my friend Lindsay sent me a card with the following verse and it is one I have held close to my heart:

"The Lord is the One who will go before you. He will be with you; He will not leave you or forsake you. Do not be afraid or discouraged." Deuteronomy 31:8 HCSB

DAY 19: God is Omniscient

God is *Omniscient*

Omni = ***all***

Science, *Latin scientia* = ***knowledge***

A few days ago we studied the *incomprehensibility* of God and the fact that His thoughts are far above ours and we will never be able to fully understand all of who He is and what He does.

I hope I am not the only crazy out there who doesn't understand why she does, says, or thinks some things. There is the age-old expression I am sure we have all used: *"He/She knows me better than I know myself!"* However, God fully understands Himself!

"For who among men knows the thoughts of a man except the spirit of the man that is in him? In the same way, no one knows the thoughts of God except the Spirit of God." 1 Corinthians 2:11 HCSB

"Do you understand how the clouds float, those wonderful works of Him who has perfect knowledge?" Job

37:16 HCSB

"God is greater than our conscience, and He knows all things." 1 John 3:20b HCSB

When trials come in our lives they might take us by surprise, but not our God. He doesn't learn — He simply knows.

"Who has directed the Spirit of the Lord,
or who gave Him His counsel?
Who did He consult with?
Who gave Him understanding
and taught Him the paths of justice?
Who taught Him knowledge
and showed Him the way of understanding?" Isaiah 40:13-14 HCSB

"Your eyes saw me when I was formless;
all my days were written in Your book and planned
before a single one of them began." Psalm 139:16 HCSB

This can be a challenge! If God knows everything and is always there, then why does He allow suffering to enter into my life? This is where we have to fall back on the *incomprehensibility* of God and trust He is allowing these things for a purpose and *"We know that all things work together for the good of those who love God: those who are called according to His purpose." Romans 8:28*

HCSB.

We will never fully understand the mind of God — but He fully understands Himself and He knows *all* things — including what it is like to endure suffering. Jesus understands suffering like no other after He died on the cross for our sins.

"For we do not have a high priest who is unable to sympathize with our weaknesses, but One who has been tested in every way as we are, yet without sin." Hebrews 4:15 HCSB

DAY 20: God is Omnipotent

God is *Omnipotent*

Omni = *all*

Potence, *Latin potens = power*

"There are no limits on God's power to do what he decides to do." ~ Wayne Grudem, Bible Doctrine

"For He spoke, and it came into being;
He commanded, and it came into existence." Psalm 33:9 HCSB

"Oh, Lord God! You Yourself made the heavens and earth by Your great power and with Your outstretched arm. Nothing is too difficult for You!" Jeremiah 32:17 HCSB

Power rests in the hands of God and was evident in Jesus during His time on earth. Recognizing His power, people would struggle through the crowds just to touch His cloak in the hope of healing:

"The whole crowd was trying to touch Him, because power was coming out from Him and healing them all." Luke 6:19 HCSB

Jesus' power over demons and darkness was witnessed,

leaving the crowds asking: *"What is this message? For He commands the unclean spirits with authority and power, and they come out!" Luke 4:36 HCSB*

God is *omnipotent* **but there are some things He cannot do!**

He cannot lie: *"in the hope of eternal life that God, who cannot lie, promised before time began." Titus 1:2 HCSB*

He cannot be tempted: *"For God is not tempted by evil, and He Himself doesn't tempt anyone." James 1:13b HCSB*

He cannot deny Himself: *"if we are faithless, He remains faithful, for He cannot deny Himself." 2 Timothy 2:13 HCSB*

God's *omnipotence* is incommunicable but we are created in His likeness and so He does grant us access to His power in order to face the trials in our lives and the work He places before us.

"For God has not given us a spirit of fearfulness, but one of power, love, and sound judgment." 2 Timothy 1:7 HCSB

In Paul's letter to the Philippians, he claims to have learned the secret to contentment and facing all circumstances he is placed in through His service to the Lord — even imprisonment — it is to do all things relying on the strength and power of the Lord.

"I am able to do all things through Him who strengthens me." Philippians 4:13 HCSB

Let's Get Real!

Although we are limited, we can access God's presence, knowledge, and power — how can you do so in your own life?

_____

_____

If you find any of God's _omni_ characteristics challenging, spend some time in prayer and listen for the comforting voice of the Lord giving you peace over your thoughts.

_____

_____

Can you think of any other characteristics of God beginning with "O"?

_____

_____

DAY 21: God is Perfectly Patient

Let's just remind ourselves of a foundational truth to remember when examining *any* of God's Characteristics --

He Is Perfect!

"God—His way is perfect" Psalm 18:30a HCSB

Perfect - in Hebrew תָּמִים tamim

Complete -- Whole -- Blameless -- Innocent -- With Integrity

This is the character of our God! But -- it is also the character He calls us to pursue. John writes in the readers of his letter 1 John saying to them:

"The one who says, 'I have come to know Him,' yet doesn't keep His commands, is a liar, and the truth is not in him. But whoever keeps His word, truly in him the love of God is perfected. This is how we know we are in Him: The one who says he remains in Him should walk just as He walked." 1 John 2:4-6 HCSB

While preaching the *Sermon on the Mount* Jesus Himself summarized the section of His sermon speaking about the law by calling His disciples to pursue *perfection* in all these areas.

"Be perfect, therefore, as your heavenly Father is perfect." Matthew 5:48 HCSB

Although God's *patience* is one of His *communicable* characteristics and we can possess it in some proportion – I have to admit it doesn't feel like it at times!

However, *patience* is one of the characteristics of God we are called to be *perfect! Patience* is part of the *Fruit of the Spirit* that should be evident in our lives.

"The Lord does not delay His promise, as some understand delay, but is patient with you, not wanting any to perish but all to come to repentance." 2 Peter 3:9 HCSB

I love some of the lessons from the Greek word translated as **perfect** in this verse. - μακροθυμέω *makrothumeó:*

Patience is:

Refusing to retaliate with anger

"A patient person shows great understanding, but a quick-tempered one promotes foolishness." Proverbs 14:29 HCSB

Persevering patiently and bravely

"You also must be patient. Strengthen your hearts, because the Lord's coming is near." James 5:8 HCSB

Enduring misfortunes and troubles

"Rejoice in hope; be patient in affliction; be persistent in prayer." Romans 12:12 HCSB

Patience is submitting to God's *perfect* timing and not trying at assert our own.

To summarize - *patience* is *love*.

Remember a couple of days ago we learned: "Our second response to God's *love* is to show *love*" and *"Every time we fail to **love** the Lord in our day we are stepping further away from who He created and commanded us to be."*

"Anyone who does not love does not know God, because God is love." 1 John 4:8

I believe 1 Corinthians 13:4-8 speaks more to *patience* than anything else -- maybe that is why it is listed first, because the rest of the passage speaks to so much of what *patience* is.

"Love is patient, love is kind.
Love does not envy,
is not boastful, is not conceited,
does not act improperly,
is not selfish, is not provoked,
and does not keep a record of wrongs.
Love finds no joy in unrighteousness
but rejoices in the truth.

It bears all things, believes all things,

hopes all things, endures all things.

Love never ends.

But as for prophecies,

they will come to an end;

as for languages, they will cease;

as for knowledge, it will come to an end."

Let's Get Real!

Do you strive for perfection in your life or do you allow the reality of true perfection being unattainable to defeat you?

Do you love others with patience? Sometimes those closest to us are the people we are most impatient with, but if patience is to be a reflection of God's love in us, and true love, then surely we should be most patient with those closest to us...?

What other characteristics of God can you think of beginning with "P"?

DAY 22: When God is Quiet...

The fact of the matter is...sometimes God is *Quiet!*

That's when we have to listen more intently.

Having slaughtered the prophets of the false god Baal, Elijah was being pursued for his life. He was met by an angel who gave him food and water, and he then journeyed for 40 days and 40 nights to Mount Horeb {1 Kings 19:1-8}. Elijah was then instructed to go and stand on the mount to hear the Lord:

"Then He said, "Go out and stand on the mountain in the Lord's presence." At that moment, the Lord passed by. A great and mighty wind was tearing at the mountains and was shattering cliffs before the Lord, but the Lord was not in the wind. After the wind there was an earthquake, but the Lord was not in the earthquake. After the earthquake there was a fire, but the Lord was not in the fire. And after the fire there was a voice, a soft whisper. When Elijah heard it, he wrapped his face in his mantle and went out and stood at the entrance of the cave. Suddenly, a voice came to him and said, "What are you doing here, Elijah?" 1 Kings 19:11-13 HCSB

Other translations use: *"sound of a gentle blowing" {NASB};* *"still small voice" {KJV}; "soft whisper" {NET}* leaving no doubt that the great and mighty noise of the Lord had stilled to a *quiet* sound that grabbed Elijah's attention. It is only after the storms and earthquakes of the Lord go *quiet* that Elijah moves to the entrance of the cave to continue listening to the voice of the Lord.

When I was a teacher in Scotland, often the most effective form of behavior management was not raising my voice, as that only served to raise the voices of the 30 strong-willed children in my class! I found if I sat down and began whispering, the class grew quiet so they could hear me!

Quietness grabs our attention, quietens our own voices, and causes us to listen!

We need to get comfortable with quiet — it is a perspective shift! I believe our culture has trained us to expect and almost feel entitled to immediate responses. We are used to affirmations, awards, recognition, and feedback {positive or constructive} being part of lives and so when don't hear words we wonder what is wrong. Our focus shifts to the words everyone around us is hearing instead of just getting comfortable with silence and leaning back on the Truth of the Word we have immediate access to at all times.

Maybe God becomes *quiet* in our lives when we have become

too comfortable and are not paying close attention to sitting in the *quiet* with Him, intent on hearing His voice.

Quietness is a test of our faith and trust in the unseen Word. All Christians saved by *Grace* through *Faith* have heard a Word from the Lord, whether through a sermon, reading the Bible, conviction...we have all had a heart prick, revelation, perspective shift, awakening. When it seems like God is being *quiet* in our lives...we use those moments to remember the Words we have heard from Him previously.

Remember when God seems to be *quiet...***He is** *never* **completely silent. Creation speaks!**

"The heavens are telling of the glory of God;
And their expanse is declaring the work of His hands." Psalm 19:1
NASB

Remember when God seems to be *quiet...***He is** *omnipresent* **and always with you!**

"Where can I go to escape Your Spirit?
Where can I flee from Your presence?
If I go up to heaven, You are there;
if I make my bed in Sheol, You are there.
If I live at the eastern horizon
or settle at the western limits,

even there Your hand will lead me;

Your right hand will hold on to me." Psalm 139:7-10 HCSB

Remember when God seem to be quiet...**He is our unchanging compassionate loving God!**

"This is why I tell you: Don't worry about your life, what you will eat or what you will drink; or about your body, what you will wear. Isn't life more than food and the body more than clothing? Look at the birds of the sky: They don't sow or reap or gather into barns, yet your heavenly Father feeds them. Aren't you worth more than they?" Matthew 6:25-26 HCSB

The reality is, God is speaking all the time, just not always in the way we expect. When Jesus was tempted He relied on the previous Words spoken by God: *"...You shall not put the Lord your God to the test...You shall worship the Lord your God, and serve Him only..."* {Matthew 4:1-11}.

He has spoken His forever and daily plan into your life through His greatest commandment:

"And He said to him, 'You shall love the Lord your God with all your heart, and with all your soul, and with all your mind.' This is the great and foremost commandment. The second is like it, 'You shall love your neighbor as yourself.'" Matthew 22:37-39 NASB

So when it seems like the Lord is being quiet *in our lives we continue to love Him and others while we:*

"Wait for the Lord;
Be strong and let your heart take courage;
Yes, wait for the Lord." Psalm 27:14 NASB

Sometimes when God is quiet **He is at His busiest working behind the scenes preparing the answer we are waiting for!**

I love this tweet quote from Bob Goff I read in an article in the Relevant Magazine[1]:

"quit waiting for God to give you a plan when you know His intent. Love God, love people, do stuff."

Let's Get Real!

Do you feel like the Lord is being quiet in your life at the moment? How can you spend time moving toward His voice to listen more intently?

_____

_____

If you are waiting for an answer from the Lord – use the time to continue to love Him, love others, and do stuff! What can you do to serve Him today?

_____

_____

Can you think of any other characteristics of God beginning with "Q"?

_____

_____

[1] http://www.relevantmagazine.com/god/what-remember-when-god-silent

DAY 23: The RIGHTEOUSNESS of God!

Wayne Grudem sums up God's *Righteousness* as this:

"God's righteousness means that God always acts in accordance with what is right and is himself the final standard of what is right."

> *"The Rock—His work is perfect;*
> *all His ways are entirely just.*
> *A faithful God, without prejudice,*
> *He is righteous and true." Deuteronomy 32:4 HCSB*

> *"I, Yahweh, speak truthfully;*
> *I say what is right." Isaiah 45:19 HCSB*

Righteous in Deuteronomy 32:4 = צַדִּיק tsaddiq

God is right and just:

- in discrimination

- condemnation

- redemption

- keeping promises

- in all his ways.

How often have you heard the words spoken to you, or spoken these words to your children or others:

Do the right thing — stay true to yourself — remember who you are.

It is part of God's moral, perfect, and Holy character to do what is right. If He did not, then He would not be staying true to who He is. He *cannot* forget. He *cannot* lie. He is faithful to His Word.

- It is because of God's righteousness that He cast Adam and Eve out of the Garden of Eden.

- It is because of God's righteousness that He destroyed the earth with a flood.

- It is because of God's righteousness that He scattered the people across the earth after the Tower of Babel.

God cannot be near sin. He is the definition of purity and He acts according to His nature.

At the time of Moses, the Ten Commandments were issued and with the building of the Tabernacle came many rules and regulations. God, in His righteousness, has to stay true to those standards and respond accordingly. He must judge and execute punishment.

"Say among the nations: "The Lord reigns.

The world is firmly established; it cannot be shaken.

He judges the peoples fairly."

Let the heavens be glad and the earth rejoice;

let the sea and all that fills it resound.

Let the fields and everything in them exult.

Then all the trees of the forest will shout for joy

before the Lord, for He is coming—

for He is coming to judge the earth.

He will judge the world with righteousness

and the peoples with His faithfulness." Psalm 96:10-13 HCSB

Grace, mercy, and compassion are also part of God's *righteous* character.

"Therefore the Lord longs to be gracious to you, And therefore He waits on high to have compassion on you. For the Lord is a God of justice; How blessed are all those who long for Him." Isaiah 30:18 NASB

When prophesying about Jesus, Isaiah stated: *"As a result of the anguish of His soul, He will see it and be satisfied; By His knowledge the Righteous One, My Servant, will justify the many, As He will bear their iniquities." Isaiah 53:11 NASB*

God's righteous character compels Him to judge and punish — but His gracious, merciful, loving character compels Him to deliver us from that punishment and shower us with forgiveness.

No one can claim to be *righteous* in their own power and ability. There is not one person who has held true to all of the standards laid out by God in the law — none!

Here the deal guys...

God *has* to judge. He has to. He is just and true and the result of our sin is death {Romans 6:23}.

BUT GOD!

He allows us to be *righteous!*

*"But now apart from the law the righteousness of God (although it is attested by the law and the prophets) has been disclosed— namely, **the righteousness of God through the faithfulness of Jesus Christ for all who believe.** For there is no distinction, for all have sinned and fall short of the glory of God. But they are **justified freely by His grace through the redemption that is in Christ Jesus.** God publicly displayed Him at His death as the mercy seat accessible through faith. This was to demonstrate his righteousness, because God in his forbearance had passed over the sins previously committed. This was also to demonstrate His righteousness in the present time, so that He would be just and the **justifier of the one who lives because of Jesus'***

faithfulness." Romans 3:21-26 NET {emphasis and
capitalization of deity pronouns mine}

- I am a sinner.
- I deserve death – Spiritual death – separation from God
  for eternity.
- God in His *righteous* nature has to pass that judgement
  upon me.
- I am a child of God.
- God loves me.
- God in His *righteous* nature loves me too much to let me
  feel His wrath and sentencing.
- He let His Son Jesus feel His wrath in my place.

"It is finished" — John 19:30

**When we are justified through faith in Christ and
the forgiveness of our sins, we are made righteous in the eyes of
our Father God!**

*"He made Him who knew no sin to be sin on our behalf, so that we
might become the righteousness of God in Him." 2 Corinthians
5:21 NASB*

*"Therefore, since we have been declared righteous by faith, we
have peace with God through our Lord Jesus Christ." Romans 5:1
HCSB*

His father Jacob gifted Joseph with a robe of many colors which made him stand out from all the others but was also a symbol of his extravagant love for his son {Genesis 37:3-4}. Through salvation, God clothes His people with a robe of righteousness as a symbol of His love to set His children apart from the rest of the world.

"I will rejoice greatly in the Lord,

My soul will exult in my God;

For He has clothed me with garments of salvation,

He has wrapped me with a robe of righteousness,

As a bridegroom decks himself with a garland,

And as a bride adorns herself with her jewels.

For as the earth brings forth its sprouts,

And as a garden causes the things sown in it to spring up,

So the Lord God will cause righteousness and praise

To spring up before all the nations." Isaiah 61:10-11 NASB

Part of the Armor we are clothed in as Christians is the Breastplate of Righteousness. The righteousness we receive from the Lord forever shields our heart and soul from death. We receive the Lord's protection through salvation.

"Stand firm therefore... having put on the breastplate of righteousness" Ephesians 6:14 NASB

Child of God, you are righteous in the eyes of your Father God in

Heaven who loves you!

Let's Get Real!

Do you live as though you are righteous in the eyes of the
Father, or do you continue to wear your past?

Why not write a prayer to the Lord today accepting His gift of a
robe and breastplate of righteousness and declaring your faith
in Him.

Can you think of any other characteristics of God beginning
with "R"?

DAY 24: God is SOVEREIGN over all!

Can I start today by just being real?! Just after I began writing about the *Sovereignty* of God an email interrupted by thoughts {note to self--switch off communications while writing!}. This email contained some information, which has the potential to become scary news for us and I felt the fingers of fear begin to take a chokehold of me.

Then I prayed.

Then I sought wise counsel and my precious friend Wendy Blight replied with these words:

"We reject fear and anxiety in the name of Jesus. God, you are bigger than ... May your peace flow through Sarah like a river, ever flooding through her and never ceasing!! You are good ALL the time."

My God -- your God -- is *Sovereign* **over all.**

"God will bring this about in His own time. He is the blessed and only Sovereign, the King of kings, and the Lord of lords," 1 Timothy 6:15 HCSB

"The Lord has established His throne in the heavens,

And His sovereignty rules over all." Psalm 103:19 NASB

God is ruler over all!

God is in control!

God is Sovereign over all things! He is the creator of all things and in Him all things are held together {Colossians 1:17}.

Sovereign over Joseph's life {read about Joseph in Genesis 37-50}

When Joseph was sold by his brothers as a slave, it was for a purpose. God was *sovereign* over Joseph's life and needed to use some, lets face it, pretty harsh circumstances to bring about the end result of Joseph being in the right place at the right time to protect the lives of His people during famine. Joseph himself was able to say to his brothers: *"As for you, you meant evil against me, but God meant it for good in order to bring about this present result, to preserve many people alive." Genesis 50:20 NASB*

Sovereign over Esther's life {Read about Esther in Esther 1-10}

A young woman, Esther, spent many years hiding her identity surrounded by people other than her own family, heritage, and beliefs. She was a modern day missionary to a country of persecution. She risked her life but God in His *sovereignty* had a plan all along to use her in order to save His people: *"Queen*

Esther answered, "If I have obtained your approval, my king, and if the king is pleased, spare my life—this is my request; and spare my people—this is my desire. For my people and I have been sold out to destruction, death, and extermination." Esther 7:3-4a HCSB

Sovereign **over Job's life {Read about Job in Job 1-42}**

Job lost everything. He lost his home and his family {Job 1:20-21}, he lost his health {Job 2:7-8}, and he suffered to the point of wishing he had died at birth {Job 3:11}. At the end of the account of Job's suffering he is recorded saying: *"Then Job replied to the Lord: I know that You can do anything and no plan of Yours can be thwarted. You asked, "Who is this who conceals My counsel with ignorance?" Surely I spoke about things I did not understand, things too wonderful for me to know. You said, "Listen now, and I will speak. When I question you, you will inform Me." I had heard rumors about You, but now my eyes have seen You. Therefore I take back my words and repent in dust and ashes." Job 42:1-6 HCSB*

With the lesson in His *sovereignty* clearly told to Job and his friends and recognition given to His control -- the Lord restored Job with twice as much as he had before {Job 42:10}.

God allows suffering in order to display His Sovereignty and miraculous power

He allowed leprosy so Jesus could heal, storms so Jesus could calm them, demonic possession so Jesus could show authority over demons, paralyzation so Jesus could rise up, blindness so Jesus could restore sight, death so Jesus could display His resurrection power {Matthew 9 and 10; John 11}.

In all things we remember and find peace in the truth of God's *sovereignty.* Even when we cannot understand {remember our God is incomprehensible at times!}, we know He is at work and:

"We know that all things work together for the good of those who love God: those who are called according to His purpose." Romans 8:28 HCSB

When I question God's *sovereignty* I need to rest in the knowledge that His *sovereign* ruling over all included His *sovereignty* over the death of His Son Jesus on the cross -- without which I would be nothing but a sinner headed for eternal punishment. Then I praise Him for His *sovereign* plan of redemption!

"Yours, Lord, is the greatness and the power and the glory and the splendor and the majesty, for everything in the heavens and on earth belongs to You. Yours, Lord, is the kingdom, and You are exalted as head over all. Riches and honor come from You, and You are the ruler of everything. Power and might are in Your hand,

and it is in Your hand to make great and to give strength to all. Now therefore, our God, we give You thanks and praise Your glorious name." 1 Chronicles 29:11-13 NASB

Let's Get Real!

Do you sometimes doubt God's sovereignty in your responses to situations? I know I do and it is an area in which I have to continually repent and declare God as being in control of my life.

_____

_____

What battle plan can you have in place when circumstances arise causing the fingers of fears to choke you?

_____

_____

Can you think of any other characteristics of God beginning with "S"?

_____

_____

DAY 25: We Can TRUST God because He is TRUE!

Jesus, in His prayer for Himself, His disciples, and all believers, just before He was arrested, prayed these words:

"This is eternal life:

that they may know You, the only true God,

and the One You have sent—Jesus Christ." John 17:3 HCSB

In some of the final moments before His crucifixion, Jesus was focused on the *truthfulness* of God.

In some of the final moments before His crucifixion, Jesus was focused on my eternal life — your eternal life — that would be achieved through Him.

We can **trust** *God because even in Jesus' moments of desperation and impending suffering – His eyes were fixed on the One True God and His plan for you and me.*

"Every word of God is pure;

He is a shield to those who take refuge in Him." Proverbs 30:5

"God is not a man, that He should lie,

Nor a son of man, that He should repent;

Has He said, and will He not do it?

Or has He spoken, and will He not make it good?" Numbers 23:19

*"Because God wanted to show His unchangeable purpose even more clearly to the heirs of the promise, He guaranteed it with an oath, so that through two unchangeable things, in which it is **impossible for God to lie**, we who have fled for refuge might have strong encouragement to seize the **hope** set before us. We have this hope as an anchor for our lives, safe and secure. It enters the inner sanctuary behind the curtain." Hebrews 6:17-19 HCSB*

We can trust God because He cannot lie and His Word is True!

"When I am afraid,

I will trust in You.

In God, whose word I praise,

in God I trust; I will not fear.

What can man do to me?" Psalm 56:3-4 HCSB

In The Treasury of David, when talking about this verse, C. H. Spurgeon writes:

*"It is a blessed fear which drives us to **trust**. Unregenerate fear drives from God, gracious fear drives to Him. If I fear man **I have only to trust God, and I have the best antidote**. To trust when there is no cause for fear is but the name of faith, but to be reliant*

upon God when occasions for alarm are abundant and pressing is the conquering faith of God's elect. Though the verse is in the form of a resolve, it became a fact in David's life; let us make it so in ours. Whether the fear arises from without or within, from past, present or future, from temporals or spirituals, from men or devils, let us maintain faith, and we shall soon recover courage."

So if God's Word and God Himself are *trustworthy* and *true*, then what can we believe? What can we rest our faith and trust in?

- God is *sovereign* and at work in the lives of all.

- God is *faithful* to His promises.

- God is *gracious, merciful, forgiving, and loves unconditionally*

We can *trust* God in all things because He works in all things. He is fighting for us and His Word is *true* when it was revealed to John in a vision:

"Then I heard a loud voice from the throne:

Look! God's dwelling is with humanity,
and He will live with them.
They will be His people,
and God Himself will be with them

and be their God.

He will wipe away every tear from their eyes.

Death will no longer exist;

grief, crying, and pain will exist no longer,

because the previous things have passed away.

Then the One seated on the throne said, "Look! I am making everything new." He also said, "Write, because these words are faithful and true." And He said to me, "It is done! I am the Alpha and the Omega, the Beginning and the End. I will give water as a gift to the thirsty from the spring of life. The victor will inherit these things, and I will be his God, and he will be My son." Revelation 21:3-7 HCSB

For the saved and redeemed Child of God there will one day be:

- No more tears.

- No more death.

- No more suffering.

- No more pain.

- Only joy!

Let's Get Real!

Do you trust God? Really trust Him? Do you trust Him in hardship and not only when you see things going to plan?

_____

_____

Write down some of the promises of God you can hold onto as Trustworthy and True to help you face the trials of life.

_____

_____

Can you think of any other characteristics of God beginning with "T"?

_____

_____

DAY 26: Only our God is UNCHANGING!

I am not too great with change which is a strange statement for me, the gal who lived immigrated at age 32 and moved 4 times in the last 3 years, to say! Truth is if you land a last-minute change on me...step back and give me 5 because I will need some time and space to process!

The truth is everything around us is changing every day and will continue to change. We will continue to have our lives rocked by changes in health, finances, bereavement, jobs, earthquakes, hurricanes, family...the attitudes and behavior of those around us will continue to cause us to bring change into our lives.

Change is real.

- Change can hurt in the form of a change of heart or the decisions made by someone close.

- Change can bring joy in the form of a new baby, job, good news.

- Change can breathe doubt when something doesn't go to plan.

- Change can leave us numb when it comes with heartbreaking news.

Change is a daily challenge we all have to face but we can face it with the strength of an *Unchanging God!*

"Long ago You established the earth,

and the heavens are the work of Your hands.

They will perish, but You will endure;

all of them will wear out like clothing.

You will change them like a garment,

and they will pass away.

But You are the same,

and Your years will never end." Psalm 102:25-27 HCSB

My address might change but my omnipresent *Unchanging God* is the same wherever I go!

"Am I a God at hand, declares the Lord, and not a God far away? Can a man hide himself in secret places so that I cannot see him? declares the Lord. Do I not fill heaven and earth? declares the Lord." Jeremiah 23:23-24 ESV

My feelings and attitude might change but my *Unchanging God* is the same yesterday, today, and forever!

"Jesus Christ is the same yesterday, today, and forever." Hebrews 13:8 HCSB

In moments when my faith wavers with the tides of change the faith of my *Unchanging God* does not!

"if we are faithless, He remains faithful, for He cannot deny Himself." 2 Timothy 2:13 HCSB

The circumstances around me might seem hopeless at times but my *Unchanging God* fill me with hope.

"Now may the God of hope fill you with all joy and peace as you believe in Him so that you may overflow with hope by the power of the Holy Spirit." Romans 15:13 HCSB

When I am tired out and feel like I have no energy to last the day I can rest in my *Unchanging God* whose energy never lacks — nor does His understanding.

"Do you not know? Have you not heard? Yahweh is the everlasting God, the Creator of the whole earth. He never grows faint or weary; there is no limit to His understanding." Isaiah 40:28 HCSB

From everlasting to everlasting, alpha to omega, in all things at all times and everywhere, the *Unchanging* grace, mercy, love, and compassion of our Lord is present all around us and within us.

Even in the midst of all the changes of life, the child of God can always be sure of one thing — the final change that will take place will bring eternal joy with the only One who is *Unchanging* — our God.

"For I, the Lord, do not change; therefore you, O sons of Jacob, are not consumed." Malachi 3:6 NASB

Let's Get Real!

Do you struggle with change? Spend some time sitting quietly and ask the Lord to reveal to you why that is? What is it about change you do not like?

_____

_____

Look up verses about our *Unchanging God* and write some out as promise prayers for those moments when change sweeps you off your feet — be grounded in the *Unchanging God.*

_____

_____

What other characteristics of God can you think of beginning with "U"?

_____

_____

DAY 27: God's VICTORY is ours to Claim!

In the beginning...

God created paradise. All was well and Adam and Eve had a problem free life and unhindered fellowship with the Lord.

But then...

"through one transgression there resulted condemnation to all men" Romans 5:18 NASB

Adam was created to be the father of mankind and so when Adam and Eve committed the first sin, the whole of mankind inherited his sin nature and as a result...

"all have sinned and fall short of the glory of God" Romans 3:23

God has allowed Satan to have some influence and control over the fallen world which is why Satan is referred to as *"the god of this world" {2 Corinthians 4:4} and "prince of the power of the air" {Ephesians 2:2}.*

Those who do not believe in the Lord and have not accepted Jesus Christ as their Savior are in the hands of Satan. When we put our trust in the Lord and believe in Him we *"escape from the snare of the devil, having been held captive by him to do his will." 2 Timothy 2:26 NASB.*

Every day we are influenced by the father of lies {John 8:44} and are hunted by the prowling lion enemy {1 Peter 5:8}.

The battle is real.

"For our battle is not against flesh and blood, but against the rulers, against the authorities, against the world powers of this darkness, against the spiritual forces of evil in the heavens." Ephesians 6:12 HCSB

But we are equipped to stand up in the battle.

"This is why you must take up the full armor of God, so that you may be able to resist in the evil day, and having prepared everything, to take your stand. Stand, therefore,

with truth like a belt around your waist,
righteousness like armor on your chest,
and your feet sandaled with readiness
for the gospel of peace.
In every situation take the shield of faith,
and with it you will be able to extinguish
all the flaming arrows of the evil one.
Take the helmet of salvation,
and the sword of the Spirit,

which is God's word.

Pray at all times in the Spirit with every prayer and request, and stay alert in this with all perseverance and intercession for all the saints." Ephesians 6:13-18 HCSB

The battle has already been won.

Scripture tells us we will have troubles in this world and I am sure we can all relate! But Scripture also tells us that we can be courageous because God has conquered the world! {John 16:33} In his vision of the end times, John saw the final picture of our *Victorious God* defeating the Devil for eternity.

"The Devil who deceived them was thrown into the lake of fire and sulfur where the beast and the false prophet are, and they will be tormented day and night forever and ever." Revelation 20:10 HCSB

One day, the one who has tormented you and me, will himself be tormented forever.

The VICTORY is ours to claim!

"You are from God, little children, and you have conquered them, because the One who is in you is greater than the one who is in the world." 1 John 4:4 HCSB

The Spirit of God lives in all Christians saved

by *grace* through *faith*.

This is the same Spirit who raised Jesus from the grave to conquer my sin, your sin, and bring life and *victory!* {Romans 8:11}

Seriously! If you are a Child of God who believes that they are a sinner in need of a Savior, and who believes that Jesus Christ *is* their Savior who took the punishment for *all* their sins — then you have the Spirit of God — the *Victorious One* living inside you!

Just as your salvation is a gift — so is the victory over the enemy!

"For whatever is born of God overcomes the world; and this is the victory that has overcome the world—our faith." 1 John 5:4 NASB

"but thanks be to God, who gives us the victory through our Lord Jesus Christ." 1 Corinthians 15:57 NASB

Our *Victorious God* shares His *victory* with His precious children who He will one day release from battle.

Let's Get Real!

What is at the front of your mind — the battle you are facing or your *Victorious God?*

_____

_____

It is hard to take our minds off the trials and hurdles in our path. Spend some time reflecting on the *Victory of the Lord* and write out a battle prayer to turn to in times of trouble.

_____

_____

What other characteristics of God can you think of beginning with "V"?

_____

_____

DAY 28: He is WORTHY of our Praise!

Worthy = deserving of, suitable for, fitting

*"The Lord is great and certainly **worthy of praise!***
No one can fathom his greatness!" Psalm 145:3 NET

On the very first day of our A to Z of God's Character study we looked at Scripture to state that Jesus is the Son of God and also God Himself. He is fully man and fully God and *"the entire fullness of God's nature dwells bodily in Christ" {Colossians 2:9 HCSB}* — including all of His characteristics! *"The Son is the radiance of God's glory and the exact expression of His nature, sustaining all things by His powerful word. After making purification for sins, He sat down at the right hand of the Majesty on high." {Hebrews 1:3 HCSB}.*

Jesus is Worthy!

"And they sang a new song, saying,

*'**Worthy are You** to take the book and to break its seals; for You were slain, and purchased for God with Your blood men from every tribe and tongue and people and nation. You have made*

them to be a kingdom and priests to our God; and they will reign upon the earth.'

Then I looked, and I heard the voice of many angels around the throne and the living creatures and the elders; and the number of them was myriads of myriads, and thousands of thousands, saying with a loud voice,

*'**Worthy is the Lamb** that was slain to receive power and riches and wisdom and might and honor and glory and blessing.'" Revelation 5:9-12 NASB*

In this vision recorded by John in the Book of Revelation, he sees Jesus {lion and lamb} being praised and called *worthy* by all of Heaven!

Why is He *Worthy* of our praise?

- God created the world and is the Creator of all things {Genesis 1:1} through Jesus! {Hebrews 1:2}

- God gave you life and every breath you take! {Isaiah 42:5}

- He performs miracles in the name of the Father — *"The works that I do in My Father's name testify about Me." John 10:25b HCSB*

- Jesus is the living water and bread to forever nourish

satisfy the soul! {John 6:35}

- He is the Shepherd and Light to guide us through our lives and rescue us from darkness! {John 10:11; John 8:12]

- He was slain — died on a cross for our sins! He is the resurrection and the life! {John 11:25-26}

- He delivered us from our sins and redeemed us into fellowship with God with the power of His blood!

- His blood is powerful enough to redeem *all* people from every nation!

- It is because of Jesus that one day those saved by His blood will be brought into the Kingdom of Heaven! He is the *only* way into Heaven! {John 14:6}

- Jesus lived as a spotless, perfect human on earth and gave an example of how we are to live! {1 Peter 2}

Worthy of our Praise!

"To praise God is to call attention to his glory." Baker's Evangelical Dictionary of Biblical Theology[1]

Praise = bless; exalt; extol; glorify; magnify; thank; confess!

Jesus is *worthy* of our full attention as we glorify His Name, magnify Him in our lives, thank Him for who He is and all He has given us, and confess Him as our Lord and Savior! It is an inherent part of who He is. Just glancing through the various titles of the A to Z of God's Character studies can't help but turn my full attention to the Lord.

I love the vision of the elders and angels praising the Lord in Heaven in Revelation. In verse 12 they proclaim: *"Worthy is the Lamb that was slain to receive power and riches and wisdom and might and honor and glory and blessing."*

Power

Riches

Wisdom

Might

Honor

Glory

Blessing

Throughout Scripture, from the very creation of the earth, which was complete in seven days, the number seven is representative of completion — perfection. There are seven "I AM" statements of Jesus in the Book of John. Seven is Divine completion and used several times in the Book of Revelation, which itself is the completion of God's plan for the world.

When all of Heaven fall down to worship and sing praises to

the Lamb who was slain it is a seven-fold song proclaim He is *worthy* of complete praise and worship!

Let's Get Real!

How do you view praise and worship? If praising the Lord is turning our full attention to who He is — we do not have to set aside time or go to a certain place — we can praise Him every moment of the day.

_____

_____

Do you truly recognize the LORD as being *worthy* of your absolute and complete worship and praise? Spend some time today reflecting on *why* He is worthy and declare it through praise.

_____

_____

What other characteristics of God can you think of beginning with "W"?

_____

_____

[1] http://www.biblestudytools.com/dictionary/praise/

DAY 29: God is our XENAGOGUE — Guide!

It took some research but I found a beautiful word beginning with "X" to describe the Character of God. Is it part of His inherent nature to be our "Xenagogue" which means to be "a Guide".

"For God, our God, is our defender forever! He guides us!" Psalm 48:14 NET

When we rely on the Lord and turn to Him for *guidance* He teaches us His Truth — *"Guide me in Your truth and teach me, for You are the God of my salvation; I wait for You all day long." Psalm 25:5 HCSB*

It is so a part of God's nature and very being to *guide* us, that every Word of Scripture itself is our *guide* — *"All Scripture is inspired by God and is profitable for teaching, for rebuking, for correcting, for training in righteousness, so that the man of God may be complete, equipped for every good work." 2 Timothy 3:16-17 HCSB*

"Your word is a lamp for my feet and a light on my path." Psalm 119:105 HCSB

He assures us we can *trust* in Him and when we do He will guide our way – *"Trust in the Lord with all your heart, and do not rely on your own understanding; think about Him in all your ways, and He will guide you on the right paths." Proverbs 3:5-6 HCSB*

The Lord was with Moses through all the plagues and eventual release of the Israelites from Egypt. He was with His people as He brought them out of Egypt and across the Red Sea into safety.

"The Lord went ahead of them in a pillar of cloud to lead them on their way during the day and in a pillar of fire to give them light at night, so that they could travel day or night. The pillar of cloud by day and the pillar of fire by night never left its place in front of the people." Exodus 13:21-22 HCSB

When our eyes are fixed upon the Lord as our *guide* **we can trust Him to go before us and behind us — to be with us through it all.**

"You have enclosed me behind and before, And laid Your hand upon me." Psalm 139:5 NASB

We are called to have *faith* in the Character of God which will in turn be our *guide* — *"For we walk by faith, not by sight" 2 Corinthians 5:7 HCSB*

Jesus is the Good Shepherd who is ready to *guide* and protect His sheep when they listen to His voice {John 10:1-17}. He is the Way, Truth, and Life *guiding* us to the Father {John 14:1-4}.

Jesus told His disciples He was sending the Holy Spirit to continue to be the *guiding* light after He departed from them.

"But the Counselor, the Holy Spirit—the Father will send Him in My name—will teach you all things and remind you of everything I have told you." John 14:26 HCSB

God's nature is to be our *guide.* He gave us the ultimate helper, His Spirit, to help us understand His *guidebook* — His Word!

Let's Get Real!

Do you turn to God for guidance in the small things as well as the big decisions of life? He wants to be our guide at all times!

_____

_____

What do you think worry about the future means about our trust and faith? If we are to walk by faith and trust God to guide our steps — should worry be an issue in our lives?

_____

_____

What other characteristics of God can you think of beginning with "X"?

_____

_____

DAY 30: YAHWEH is who God is!

Yahweh is one of the most beautiful sounding names and reveals more about God's character than simply being a name. *Yahweh* is the very essence of who God is.

God revealed His Name as *Yahweh* to Moses. It is the Name He gives to Himself -- it is how He defines Himself.

*"God also said to Moses, "Say this to the Israelites: **Yahweh**, the God of your fathers, the God of Abraham, the God of Isaac, and the God of Jacob, has sent me to you. This is My name forever; this is how I am to be remembered in every generation." Exodus 3:15*

"this name stresses God as the independent and self-existent God of revelation and redemption" {Bible.org}[1]

Yahweh is always written *L⬚R⬚ {small caps}* in the Bible

One of my favorite discoveries while looking into *Yahweh* was from John Piper and I will let him tell you:

Then in the fullness of time, Yahweh came into the world to seek and save the lost. The angel said to Joseph, "You shall call his name Jesus, for he will save his people from their sins" (Matthew 1:21). Jesus is an English transliteration of the Greek Iesoun. And this in turn is a Greek transliteration of the Hebrew Joshua. And Joshua is a combination of Yah and "salvation" or "save". It means "Yahweh saves."[2]

How awesome is that!!! The very name of Jesus means **Yahweh** saves. I have tears in my eyes typing these words. When I call upon the name of Jesus, I am crying out to **"Yahweh saves"**. God's redemptive plan came to life in and through Jesus and continues to work in my life every day.

One day every knee will bow down and declare Jesus is *LⱭRⱭ* -- *Yahweh saved.* {Isaiah 45:23; Philippians 2:11}

Yahweh saves

Yahweh redeems

Jesus

The name *Yahweh* is often combined with another word to create a deeper meaning and revelation of God's character. Here are just a few descriptions of *Yahweh*.

- *Yahweh-Jireh* — He is our *provider* — *"And Abraham named that place The LORD will Provide, so today it is said: 'It will be provided on the LORD's* mountain.'" *Genesis 22:14 HCSB*

- *Yahweh-Rapha* — He is our *healer* — *"For I am Yahweh who heals you." Exodus 15:26b HCSB*

- *Yahweh-M'Kaddesh* — He makes us *Holy* — *"I am the LORD who sanctifies you." Leviticus 20:8 NASB*

- *Yahweh-Shalom* — He is a God of *Peace* — *"Then Gideon built an altar there to the LORD and named it The LORD is Peace." Judges 6:24 NASB*

- **Yahweh-Elohim** — *LORD God* — *"the LORD God made earth and heaven."*

- *Yahweh-Rohi* — He is our *Shepherd and guide* — *"The LORD is my shepherd" Psalm 23:1 NASB*

So whenever you see the word **LORD** in small caps, pause for a moment and reflect on the truth of God's Name. The Name He gave Himself. **LORD is t**he Name that identifies so much of who He is and His character. When I use the name *Yahweh* I feel like I am speaking to God on a more personal level.

Let's Get Real!

I know this is a study of the character of God but His Names define so much of His character. Which of the combined names mean most to you in your life at the moment?

Spend some time studying the Names of God today and discover more of who your Father God — Yahweh — is to you personally.

What other characteristics of God can you think of beginning with "Y"?

---

[1] https://bible.org/article/names-god

[2] http://www.desiringgod.org/articles/yahweh-is-the-sweetest-name-i-know

DAY 31: God is ZEALOUS for His People!

To be *zealous* is to be filled with a passionate desire for a cause. It is to be so eager, intense, and fervent about a cause that you cannot be anything other than fully devoted and committed to it's completion.

God is Zealous

God's redemptive plan came into effect after the first sin took place in the Garden of Eden. Since then He has been showering His *grace*, *mercy*, and *forgiveness* upon His people. Every day He shows His *faithfulness* by showing up in our lives to *deliver* us from the sins we continually fall into.

Nothing can take God's eyes of His eternal salvation and redemptive plan for His people.

God's *zealous* nature also means that one day He will judge all people.

"Lord, Your hand is lifted up to take action,
but they do not see it.
*They will see Your **zeal** for Your people,*

and they will be put to shame.

The fire for Your adversaries will consume them!" Isaiah 26:11

God's *zeal* is linked to His jealous nature, which we discussed earlier in this study.

> *We are programmed to view jealousy as a negative trait and in human terms it is! When we hear the word **jealous** our minds run to the feelings of envy leading to rivalry and bitter thought. However, there is such a thing as Godly **jealousy.***

> *"For I am jealous for you with a godly jealousy; for I betrothed you to one husband, so that to Christ I might present you as a pure virgin." 2 Corinthians 11:2 NASB*

> *Paul was so passionate about the salvation of the people of the church of Corinth that he described his desire to belong to Christ alone as **jealousy.** He didn't want the people to be influenced by and snatched away, in thought or deed, by the deception and false teaching.*

> *"But I am afraid that, as the serpent deceived Eve by his craftiness, your minds will be led astray from the simplicity and purity of devotion to Christ. For if one comes and preaches another Jesus whom we have not preached, or you receive a different spirit which you have not received,*

or a different gospel which you have not accepted, you bear this beautifully." 2 Corinthians 11:3-4 NASB

Godly *jealousy* **is when our hearts are stirred to action in the Spiritual battle over souls.**

God's zealous nature is all sufficient

Due to God's *faithfulness*, His *zealous* nature can be trusted to accomplish what He wills. He is *jealous* for the souls of His children. There is a phrase repeated in Scripture, each time in reference to His salvation plan and also His final judgement for those who refuse to acknowledge Him as Lord.

"The zeal of the Lord of Hosts will accomplish this." {2 Kings 19:31, Isaiah 9:7; Isaiah 37:32}

The Lord's *zealous* **nature means He is fully committed to accomplishing His eternal salvation and redemptive plan for His people.**

What is our response?

We are part of His plan! God's *zealous* nature is one of His communicable characteristics He desires us to have. In the passage titled: *"Marks of a True Christian"* in many Bibles {Romans 12:9-21}, Paul instructs the people:

"Do not lag in zeal, be enthusiastic in spirit, serve the

Lord." Romans 12:11 NET

As Christians we are called to be zealous in our Christian attitude and service to the Lord!

Zealousness comes with a sidekick...humility! For as passionate, eager, and intense we are to be about our call as Christians — we must be humble and not boast in our works or in ourselves.

"But it is from Him that you are in Christ Jesus, who became God-given wisdom for us—our righteousness, sanctification, and redemption, in order that, as it is written: The one who boasts must boast in the Lord." 1 Corinthians 1:30-31 HCSB

Our *zealous* nature can easily be misdirected toward things of this world; however, the work we are called to be *zealous* over is the work God has prepared for us. We don't create or find it. Godly *zeal* is to be devoted to our service to the Lord, which is nothing of our own doing — it is all from Him and only possible because of His *grace* toward us. The work we are called to be *zealous* over is an honor we do not deserve.

"For by grace you have been saved through faith, and that not of yourselves; it isthe gift of God, not of works, lest anyone should boast. For we are His workmanship, created in Christ Jesus for good works, which God prepared beforehand that we should walk in them." Ephesians 2:8-10 NKJV

God's desire for our *zeal* is for is to be infectious and stir the hearts of those around us to turn to Christ. When Paul wrote to the church in Corinth he indicated the Lord's pleasure when he said: *"For I know your eagerness, and I brag about you to the Macedonians: "Achaia has been prepared since last year," and your zeal has stirred up most of them." 2 Corinthians 9:2 HCSB*

Lord, may my *zeal* for the ministry you allow me to be part of stir the hearts of many.

Let's Get Real!

Do you have a zealous nature toward the work of the Lord?

_____

_____

How can we balance our zeal and humility?

_____

_____

What other characteristics of God can you think of beginning with "Z"?

_____

_____

A Prayer and a Thank You!

Father God, *Yahweh*, You alone are *Worthy* and I praise You for who You are. You are the *Eternal, Everlasting, Alpha* and *Omega, Beginning* and the *End*. I praise You for Your *Creation* and thank You for choosing to *create* me in Your image. Lord, I thank You for Your *Ever Present, Unchanging, Faithfulness* toward Your people.

Lord, I thank You for being *Jealous* over me. Lord, I do not deserve Your *Grace, Mercy,* and *Forgiveness* and yet, with *Compassion* You are *Patient* and continue to show me Your *Love* by *Delivering* me from my sinful nature. Lord, I deserve punishment, yet You clothe me with Your *Righteousness.* I deserve to carry the labels of my sin, yet You remove them and *Rename* me as Chosen, Beloved, Forgiven, Free, Child of God. Thank You.

Thank You, Lord, for sending Your Son *Jesus* to live a *Perfect Sinless* life and be an example of true *Beauty* and *Holiness* to Your children. Thank You for the *Victory* You sealed on the cross. Lord, I thank You for being *Zealous* in Your pursuit of me, not giving up on me when I failed to see *Truth* and *Light.* Lord, when I feel despair, You bring *Hope.* When it seems like everything is going wrong and I cannot understand my life, I can *Trust* that You do and You are with me as my *Faithful Guide*. You never leave me. You know everything I am facing at all times, and even when it seems like You are *Quiet,* You are there drawing me closer to hear Your voice. You are *Sovereign* Lord and I can trust in Your plan for my life, knowing You are at work for good.

Lord, You are the *Divine King of Kings* and *Lord of Lords*. One day I will join with the angels in Heaven singing *"Holy, holy holy!"* and *"Worthy is the Lamb that was slain to receive power and riches and wisdom and might and honor and glory and blessing"* and until then I will continue to trust, thank, and praise You, declaring Your Name among the Nations. In Jesus Name, Amen.

Thank you for joining me on this journey through the A to Z of God's Character. If you have enjoyed this study I would appreciate your review on Amazon. My prayer for you is that you would continue to dig deeper into Scripture and learn even more about our Father God and His Son Jesus and your love for Him would deepen.

I would like to invite you to keep in touch through my website at **www.sarahtravis.org** - sign up to receive a free gift.

I have also compiled all the worship songs from the study into a YouTube playlist, which you can find at: http://ow.ly/UP518

I am also very excited to let you know that my first full-length book will be released in late Spring 2016!

"From Longing to Belonging: Finding Purpose on Your Journey to Eternity"

From Longing to Belonging will track my story of immigration and take the reader on a journey from salvation to citizenship in Heaven. Personal testimony will be interspersed with Biblical teaching and practical instruction on how we are called to live as God's children in this world with the purpose of bringing glory to His Name.

ABOUT THE AUTHOR

My name is Sarah Travis and I am a writer who loves to share my love of Christ and the Truth of Scripture with the world.

I am Scottish born and bred, but the Lord brought me to the US to meet and marry my wonderful husband Jason. I struggled through my 20s failing to understand why I was single and couldn't find *"The One."* I can now see that I wasn't ready! God hadn't finished preparing me to meet him...or maybe He needed more time to prepare him for meeting me!!

I am thankful for my single years which allowed me to venture out into the world on missions trips to France, Mexico, South Africa, and Knoxville, Tennessee. I learned so much about myself and the Lord through these times. It was toward the end of ten months in Tennessee that the Lord introduced me to Jason and started me on a new journey...one that now has me married and living in the U.S.

"The heart of man plans his ways, but the Lord establishes his steps." Proverbs 16:9 ESV

Made in the USA
Columbia, SC
26 February 2020

88416715R00078